APPIN   SHOW

Stalker Cottage

12.8.95

FIRST PRIZE.......................

....

LYNN BEDFORD HALL'S

BISCUITS & BREADS

LYNN BEDFORD HALL'S

BISCUITS & BREADS

PHOTOGRAPHY BY ANTHONY JOHNSON

NATIONAL

This edition first published in the UK in 1994 by National,
an imprint of New Holland (Publishers) Ltd
37 Connaught Street, London W2 2AZ

ISBN 1 85974 000 6

Editors: Elizé Lübbe and Alison Leach
Designer: Petal Palmer
Illustrator: Tobie Beele
Photographer: Anthony Johnson
Styling: Vo Pollard

Typesetting by BellSet
Reproduction by Unifoto (Pty) Ltd
Printed and bound in Singapore by Tien Wah Press (Pte.) Ltd

CONTENTS

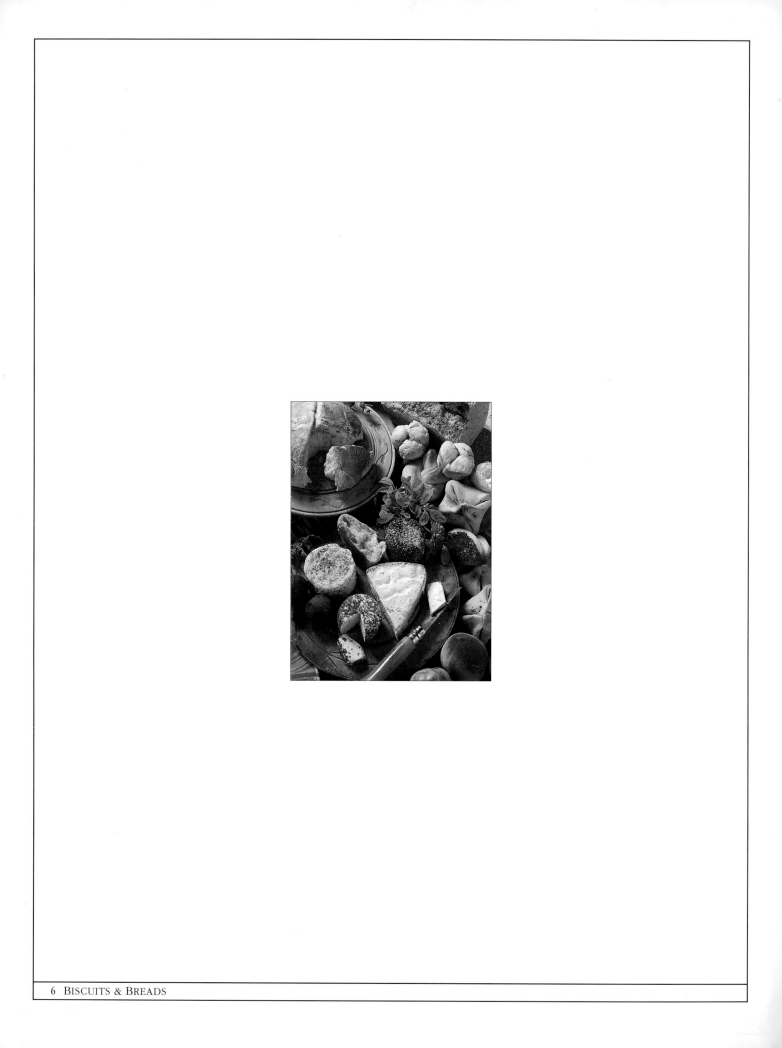

FOREWORD

This book is the result of a very long baking affair. For months I have mixed and kneaded, creamed and rolled, proved and cut, and it has left me – not only a little floury – but also convinced that home-baking should definitely be put back on the culinary map.

There are, however, so many good biscuits and breads on the market these days, that many people have lost the urge to make their own. This is a pity, because not only is baking both relaxing and enjoyable, but nothing out of a packet can match the nose-twitching aroma of freshly baked bread, scones and muffins.

Bread-baking, in particular, can become an addictive pastime. Kneading is wonderfully therapeutic and gets rid of a lot of aggression on the days when you're feeling uptight.

Baking biscuits and rusks, quick breads, scones and muffins can be equally satisfying and is a means to endless creativity. For example, in certain recipes I have substituted wholewheat flour for some of the cake flour. This does mean that the end product will be a little heavier and different in texture from the refined versions, but rather more wholesome and in line with the present swing to less processed ingredients. You will probably also notice that I have cut down a little on sugar and salt, proving that one can jiggle recipes to adapt to one's own tastes and convictions, and I am sure you will find yourself adding many personal touches to my ideas.

In most recipes you will not have to use a scale. Quantities are such that they can easily be measured with a metric cup or spoon, and even when butter is used, the recipes almost always require a block simply to be cut into convenient halves or quarters.

I have, without exception, used extra large eggs, and I suggest you do the same, else you might end up with too little liquid and, therefore, a different result.

For creaming and mixing most biscuits and sweet loaves, I have used a hand-held Philips three-speed electric beater. I cannot guarantee the same results if you try creaming with a wooden spoon. Using an electric beater is quick, easy and thorough. However, I have rarely used the dough hooks for bread, simply because I think it is important to develop a personal relationship with your dough. If you feel and knead it with your hands it becomes, in today's idiom, user-friendly, and you will soon learn to tell when the right consistency has been reached.

I hope, with this book, to help define the trend back to home cooking. Even if it is only on special, less pressurized days, homecooks all over are definitely displaying a predilection for presenting their families with bakes that didn't start out pre-wrapped in a trolley. I've done it, and so can you, and while test-baking for this book there were many occasions on which I called my family to come and peer in through the glass oven door to watch whatever it was rising, spreading and browning. Which proves that baking can become a communal experience and when the results are good, the reward is a companionable sharing.

And finally, all that is left to be said is to wish you the best of baking, and happy munching!

Lynn Bedford Hall

BISCUITS & COOKIES

SPICE COOKIES

Granny used mutton fat rather than butter and left her dough to stand overnight, followed by a long session of rolling and cutting out little circles with a glass. Granny had lots of time, and would doubtless have disapproved of these easy spice 'n' slice cookies, using everyday ingredients, but do try them – they're so delicious.

150 g (5 oz) plain flour or white bread flour
150 g (5 oz) brown bread flour
5 ml (1 tsp) baking powder
pinch of salt
2.5 ml (½ tsp) bicarbonate of soda
5 ml (1 tsp) ground mixed spice
5 ml (1 tsp) ground cinnamon
1.25 ml (¼ tsp) ground cloves
2.5 ml (½ tsp) ground ginger
125 g (4 oz) soft butter
100 g (3½ oz) caster sugar
100 g (3½ oz) demerara sugar
1 egg
30 ml (2 tbsp) sweet sherry

Sift both flours with baking powder, salt, bicarbonate of soda and spices. Return any bran left in the sieve. Cream butter and slowly add both sugars, beating well. Beat egg with sherry and beat into butter mixture with 5 ml (1 tsp) of the flour mixture, then mix in remaining flour mixture to make a soft dough. Shape into two 3-cm (1¼-in) diameter sausages. Wrap in greaseproof paper and chill for about 1 hour. Using a sharp knife, slice into 5-mm (¼-in) thick rounds and place on oiled baking trays, leaving room for spreading. Bake at 160°C (325°F, gas 3) for 15 minutes, then remove to wire racks to cool and crisp.
Makes about 70

Bright and dainty little Coconut Cherry Stars (page 19) and deliciously crisp Lemon Sesame Snaps.

NUT AND OAT COOKIES

Simple, old-fashioned buttery biscuits.

250 g (9 oz) soft butter
200 g (7 oz) caster sugar
few drops vanilla essence
1 egg, beaten
250 g (9 oz) plain flour
45 ml (3 tbsp) cornflour
pinch of salt
10 ml (2 tsp) baking powder
90 g (3 oz) rolled oats
100 g (3½ oz) finely chopped pecan nuts

Cream butter, sugar and vanilla. Add egg and mix well. Sift flour, cornflour, salt and baking powder and add. Mix until combined and then add oats and nuts. Knead with your hands until mixture forms a ball. Pinch off small pieces, roll into balls, and place on oiled baking trays. Press down lightly with a fork and bake at 180°C (350°F, gas 4) on middle shelf of oven for 20 minutes. Cool on a wire rack.
Makes about 48

BROWNIES

There are several versions of this American favourite; this one is like a light, thinly crusted chocolate cake.

3 eggs
150 g (5 oz) caster sugar
45 ml (3 tbsp) demerara sugar
100 g (3½ oz) plain chocolate, broken up
125 g (4 oz) butter
150 g (5 oz) plain flour
5 ml (1 tsp) baking powder
pinch of salt
125 g (4 oz) chopped walnuts or pecan nuts
few drops vanilla essence

Beat the eggs and sugars together until thick and pale. Melt the chocolate and butter together over very low heat. Beat the chocolate into the egg mixture. Sift the flour, baking powder and salt together, add to egg mixture and stir until combined. Stir in nuts and vanilla. Pour into an oiled, 25 x 20-cm (10 x 8-in) baking tin and bake at 180°C (350°F, gas 4) for 35 minutes until just firm and starting to crack round the edges. Be careful not to overbake. Cut into squares and leave to cool in tin. These brownies keep well.
Makes about 36

HINT
● *Keep biscuits crisp by storing them in airtight containers with a sprinkling of sugar between the layers.*

LEMON SESAME SNAPS

Deliciously crisp, brown biscuits. Toasting brings out the flavour of sesame seeds: spread them out on a large baking tray and place in oven, either preheated, or when you turn it on prior to baking. Remove when golden brown, watching carefully as they burn easily.

125 g (4 oz) soft butter
few drops vanilla essence
75 g (2½ oz) caster sugar
10 ml (2 tsp) finely grated lemon rind
25 ml (5 tsp) honey
75 g (2½ oz) white bread flour
pinch of salt
2.5 ml (½ tsp) bicarbonate of soda
75 g (2½ oz) wholewheat flour
60 g (2 oz) toasted sesame seeds

Cream the butter, vanilla, sugar, lemon rind and honey together. Sift white bread flour, salt and bicarbonate of soda together. Mix into the creamed mixture, then add wholewheat flour and sesame seeds. Combine well to a soft dough. Shape into a ball, pinch off small pieces, roll into balls and place on oiled baking trays, leaving room for spreading. Press down with tines of a fork, making a criss-cross pattern, and bake at 180°C (350°F, gas 4) for 12 minutes. Leave on tray for 1 minute to crisp, then transfer to a wire rack to cool.
Makes about 30

BASIC BUTTER BISCUITS

Make several batches and flavour the biscuits in a variety of ways – they're very quick to mix with the help of a hand-held electric beater.

125 g (4 oz) soft butter
150 g (5 oz) caster sugar
1 egg, lightly beaten
few drops vanilla essence
250 g (9 oz) white bread flour
5 ml (1 tsp) cream of tartar
2.5 ml (½ tsp) bicarbonate of soda

Cream butter and sugar until light, add egg and vanilla and beat. Sift dry ingredients and add. Mix to a soft dough and then shape into a ball with your hands. Pinch off walnut-sized pieces and place on oiled or non-stick baking tray, leaving room for spreading. Press down lightly with the tines of a fork and bake on the middle shelf of the oven at 180°C (350°F, gas 4) for 12 minutes, or until pale beige. Cool on a wire rack.
Makes about 30

VARIATIONS
Coffee Pecan Butter Biscuits
Substitute demerara sugar for the caster sugar. Beat egg lightly with 15 ml (1 tbsp) instant coffee granules and the vanilla essence, until coffee has dissolved. Add 45 g (1½ oz) finely chopped pecan nuts to the dough and top each biscuit with a pecan piece.

Lemon Peel Butter Biscuits
Cream butter and sugar with 5 ml (1 tsp) finely grated lemon rind. Use only 125 g (4 oz) white bread flour when sifting, then add 125 g (4 oz) wholewheat flour and 45 g (1½ oz) finely chopped mixed peel. Top each biscuit with a sultana.

Chocolate Butter Biscuits
Sift 10 ml (2 tsp) cocoa powder with the dry ingredients and add 45 g (1½ oz) grated plain chocolate to the dough. Press a chocolate chip into the top of each biscuit.

MUNCHIES

Knobbly, wholesome cookies.

60 g (2 oz) self-raising flour
5 ml (1 tsp) ground cinnamon
125 g (4 oz) wholewheat flour
150 g (5 oz) caster sugar
150 ml (¼ pint) oil
2 eggs
75 g (2½ oz) rolled oats
150 g (5 oz) mixed dried fruit
45 g (1½ oz) desiccated coconut

Sift self-raising flour and cinnamon, then mix in wholewheat flour. Whisk together sugar, oil and eggs. Add to dry ingredients together with oats, fruit and coconut. Mix very well to a soft dough. Push large teaspoonfuls off on to oiled baking trays and bake at 180°C (350°F, gas 4) for 18 minutes. Using a spatula, transfer to wire racks to cool and crisp.
Makes about 40

COCONUT LEMON CRISPIES

Pale gold, crunchy little discs.

100 ml (3½ fl oz) oil
150 g (5 oz) caster sugar
7.5 ml (1½ tsp) finely grated lemon rind
1 egg
250 g (9 oz) white bread flour
2.5 ml (½ tsp) baking powder
pinch of salt
90 g (3 oz) desiccated coconut
extra caster sugar

Place oil, sugar and lemon rind in a deep rather than a wide mixing bowl, and beat very well. Add egg and beat until

NOTE
● *Butter biscuits should always be baked on the middle shelf of the oven to avoid browned bottoms, therefore it is best to bake them in relays.*

mixture is creamy and yellow. Sift together flour, baking powder and salt, add to creamed mixture and mix well, then beat in coconut. Roll into balls and press flat between your palms. Dip tops in extra caster sugar and place on oiled baking trays, sugar side up, leaving room for spreading. Bake at 180°C (350°F, gas 4) for 15 minutes until just browning around the edges. Cool on a wire rack.
Makes about 30

BISCUIT PRESS COOKIES

This dough keeps its shape well and may be used to make any design, but is particularly attractive made into daisy shapes with a biscuit press, with half a glacé cherry then pressed into the centre. Alternatively, sprinkle with cinnamon-flavoured sugar [mix 2.5 ml (½ tsp) ground cinnamon with 5 ml (1 tsp) caster sugar], or top with finely chopped almonds, pressed in lightly. The dough may also be flavoured with grated lemon or orange rind, or the biscuits may be sandwiched together using vanilla butter icing.

125 g (4 oz) soft butter
100 g (3½ oz) caster sugar
1 egg
few drops vanilla essence
225 g (8 oz) plain flour
45 ml (3 tbsp) cornflour
pinch of salt

Cream butter and sugar. Beat the egg and vanilla together and add. Mix well and then add flour sifted with cornflour and salt. Combine well to a soft dough and then press into a ball with your hands, rather like shortbread. Fill the biscuit press and press out on to lightly oiled baking trays, not too close, because although the mixture does not contain any raising agent, the biscuits spread slightly as the butter melts. Bake at 200°C (400°F, gas 6) for 12-15 minutes until pale beige in colour. Cool on a wire rack.
Makes 30-36

FROM THE BACK: *Chocolate Cookies; Coconut Lemon Crispies; Date Knobs; Biscuit Press Cookies.*

CHOCOLATE COOKIES

There are many versions of this favourite American cookie. Chips usually retain their shape, while chopped chocolate melts in the baking.

125 g (4 oz) soft butter
60 ml (4 tbsp) demerara sugar
60 ml (4 tbsp) caster sugar
1 egg
few drops vanilla essence
2.5 ml (½ tsp) bicarbonate of soda
10 ml (2 tsp) hot water
200 g (7 oz) plain flour
pinch of salt
10 ml (2 tsp) cocoa powder
100 g (3½ oz) plain chocolate
45-60 g (1½-2 oz) chopped walnuts
or pecan nuts

Cream butter and both sugars until light. Beat egg with vanilla and add, mixing well. Stir in bicarbonate of soda dissolved in hot water. Sift in flour, salt and cocoa. Combine well. Chop chocolate in food processor and add together with nuts, mixing to a softish dough. Then either pinch off small balls and flatten between your palms before placing on oiled baking trays, or push off rough mounds from tip of teaspoon. Bake at l80˚C (350˚F, gas 4) for 20 minutes. Cool on a wire rack.
Makes about 36

DATE KNOBS

Crisp little cakes, stuffed with dates.

PASTRY
250 g (9 oz) plain flour
45 ml (3 tbsp) cornflour
45 ml (3 tbsp) icing sugar
175 g (6 oz) chilled butter
1 egg
few drops vanilla essence
extra icing sugar

FILLING
250 g (9 oz) stoned dates, chopped
5 ml (1 tsp) lemon juice
45 ml (3 tbsp) water
30 g (1 oz) chopped walnuts

Gently heat dates, lemon juice and water until dates can be mashed with a wooden spoon. Add nuts and leave to cool.

Sift dry ingredients. Rub in butter. Beat egg and vanilla and add. Mix well. Knead into a ball – do not add any liquid. Roll out thinly on a floured board and cut into 5-7.5-cm (2-3-in) rounds. Re-roll trimmings until all the dough has been used. Place a heaped spoon of filling in the middle of a round, cover with a second round and seal edges with a fork. Prick each top twice. Place on oiled baking tray and bake at 180˚C (350˚F, gas 4) for 18-20 minutes or until pale gold. Remove to a wire rack and dredge with sifted icing sugar.
Makes about 14

COCONUT CURRANT SNAPS

A typical cookie-tin biscuit, economical and easy.

125 g (4 oz) soft butter
150 g (5 oz) caster sugar
1 egg
few drops vanilla essence
250 g (9 oz) self-raising flour
pinch of salt
90 g (3 oz) desiccated coconut
75 g (2½ oz) currants
extra caster sugar

Cream butter and sugar. Mix in egg beaten with vanilla. Sift flour with salt and add to creamed mixture together with coconut. Finally mix in currants. Knead to a ball, then pinch off small pieces and roll into balls. Press flat between your palms, dip tops in extra caster sugar and place on oiled baking trays, leaving room for spreading. Bake at 180°C (350°F, gas 4) for 15 minutes until just beginning to brown. Cool on wire racks.
Makes about 50

MELTING MOMENTS

125 g (4 oz) soft butter
100 g (3½ oz) caster sugar
1 egg, lightly beaten
few drops vanilla essence
200 g (7 oz) self-raising flour
pinch of salt
45 g (1½ oz) bran flakes or
cornflakes, coarsely crushed

Cream butter and sugar. Add egg and vanilla and beat well. Sift flour with salt and add. Mix thoroughly to a soft ball, then pinch off small pieces, roll into balls and roll in crushed cereal. Arrange on oiled baking trays, leaving room for spreading, and press down lightly with a fork. Bake on middle shelf of oven (as they brown quickly on the bottom) at 180°C (350°F, gas 4) for 15 minutes. Cool on a wire rack.
Makes about 30

CARROT AND COCONUT JUMBLES

Big, chewy and wholesome.

125 g (4 oz) soft butter
200 g (7 oz) demerara sugar
125 g (4 oz) wholewheat flour
125 g (4 oz) plain flour
90 g (3 oz) desiccated coconut
90 g (3 oz) rolled oats
185 g (6½ oz) coarsely grated carrots
5 ml (1 tsp) bicarbonate of soda
pinch of salt
10 ml (2 tsp) ground cinnamon
2.5 ml (½ tsp) ground nutmeg
75 g (2½ oz) sultanas or
seedless raisins
2 eggs, lightly beaten
few drops vanilla essence
125 ml (4 fl oz) oil

Cream butter and sugar. Add flours, coconut, oats, carrots, bicarbonate of soda, salt, spices and sultanas or raisins. Beat together eggs, vanilla and oil. Add to creamed mixture and mix very well – use an electric beater – mixture will eventually form a soft dough. Push heaped teaspoonfuls off on to lightly oiled baking trays, leaving room for spreading, and press down lightly with a fork. Bake at 180°C (350°F, gas 4) for 20 minutes. Stand for 1 minute to crisp, then use a spatula to remove to wire racks to cool.
Makes about 48

WHOLEWHEAT, HONEY AND COCONUT CRISPS

Caramel-coloured, crunchy biscuits.

125 g (4 oz) butter, melted
25 ml (5 tsp) honey
75 g (2½ oz) demerara sugar
150 g (5 oz) wholewheat flour
pinch of salt
2.5 ml (½ tsp) bicarbonate of soda
10 ml (2 tsp) hot water
45 g (1½ oz) desiccated coconut
few drops vanilla essence

Mix melted butter with honey, sugar, flour and salt. Add bicarbonate of soda dissolved in hot water. Mix in coconut and vanilla. Combine thoroughly until mixture forms a soft ball. Pinch off small pieces and roll into balls. Place on ungreased baking trays, leaving room for spreading. Press down lightly with a fork and bake at 180°C (350°F, gas 4) for 12-14 minutes until a rich brown colour. Cool on a wire rack.
Makes about 28

FLORENTINES

A thin, lacy biscuit with dried fruit and nuts, coated with chocolate on one side.

60 g (2 oz) soft butter
60 ml (4 tbsp) caster sugar
25 ml (5 tsp) sifted plain flour
45 g (1½ oz) chopped almonds
12 glacé cherries, chopped
45 ml (3 tbsp) chopped sultanas
2 knobs preserved ginger, chopped
45 ml (3 tbsp) chopped mixed peel
100 g (3½ oz) plain chocolate

Cream butter and sugar well. Fold in flour. Add almonds and fruit. Spoon large teaspoonfuls, far apart, on to baking trays, preferably non-stick but otherwise oiled and dusted with cornflour. Flatten lightly with the back of a spoon. Bake at 180°C (350°F, gas 4) for about 10 minutes or until browned with lacy edges. Remove from oven and, using a spoon, push lightly into neat circles. Using a spatula, remove carefully to a wire rack to cool. Melt chocolate very gently over simmering water – do not allow it to get too hot – and spread evenly over flat side of each cooled biscuit. Run a fork through the chocolate as it hardens to make the characteristic wavy pattern. When cold and set, store in airtight container.
Makes about 14

COCONUT ALMOND CRISPS

Big, crunchy cookies.

125 g (4 oz) soft butter
150 g (5 oz) caster sugar
few drops vanilla essence
1 egg, lightly beaten
250 g (9 oz) self-raising flour
pinch of salt
75 g (2½ oz) desiccated coconut
60 g (2 oz) finely chopped toasted
almonds

Cream butter, sugar and vanilla until light. Add egg and beat. Sift in flour and salt and mix well. Add coconut and almonds and knead to a soft ball. Pinch off small pieces, roll into balls and place on oiled baking trays, leaving plenty of room for spreading. Press twice with the tines of a fork, making a criss-cross pattern, and bake at 180°C (350°F, gas 4) for 20 minutes or until a deep beige colour. Cool on wire racks.
Makes about 40

VANILLA CONDENSED MILK DROPS

250 g (9 oz) soft butter
75 g (2½ oz) caster sugar
200 g (7 oz) canned condensed milk
375 g (13 oz) plain flour
10 ml (2 tsp) baking powder
pinch of salt
few drops vanilla essence

Cream butter and sugar. Beat in condensed milk. Sift flour, baking powder and salt and add to creamed mixture. Finally add vanilla and mix to a soft dough. Push small mounds off tip of teaspoon on to oiled or non-stick baking tray. Flatten with the tines of a fork, in a criss-cross pattern. Sprinkle lightly with cinnamon-flavoured sugar if preferred. Bake at 180°C (350°F, gas 4) for 15 minutes or until just beginning to brown. Cool on a wire rack.
Makes about 54

FROM THE BACK: *Carrot and Coconut Jumbles; Melting Moments; Wholewheat, Honey and Coconut Crisps.*

FROM THE TOP: *Spiced Sultana Slices; Bran Flake Crisps; Coconut Slices.*

ONE-BOWL RAISIN AND BRAN BARS

125 g (4 oz) self-raising flour
150 g (5 oz) caster sugar
90 g (3 oz) desiccated coconut
125 g (4 oz) seedless raisins or sultanas
45 ml (3 tbsp) mixed peel
75 ml (5 tbsp) sunflower seeds
60 g (2 oz) soft butter, diced
100 ml (3½ fl oz) oil
1 egg, beaten
45 g (1½ oz) bran flakes
few drops vanilla essence

Put ingredients in above order into large mixing bowl. Using an electric beater, beat until thoroughly combined. Spread evenly into a lightly oiled, 23-cm (9-in) square baking tin. Bake on middle shelf of oven at 180°C (350°F, gas 4) for about 30 minutes until firm and well browned. Cut into bars and cool in tin.
Makes about 18 large bars

SOURED CREAM SPICE BISCUITS

250 g (9 oz) soft butter
5 ml (1 tsp) ground cinnamon
5 ml (1 tsp) ground mixed spice
1.25 ml (¼ tsp) grated nutmeg
400 g (14 oz) demerara sugar
1 egg, lightly beaten
125 ml (4 fl oz) soured cream
500 g (18 oz) plain flour
2.5 ml (½ tsp) bicarbonate of soda
1.25 ml (¼ tsp) salt

Cream butter with spices. Slowly beat in sugar. Beat in egg and cream. Sift flour with bicarbonate of soda and salt. Add to creamed mixture and combine to a soft dough, then shape into a ball with your hands. Pinch off small pieces and roll into balls, flouring hands when necessary. Place on oiled baking trays and press down with fork, making a criss-cross pattern. Bake on middle shelf of oven at 180°C (350°F, gas 4) for 15 minutes. Cool on a wire rack.
Makes about 72

WHEAT GERM AND MUESLI CRISPS

60 g (2 oz) soft butter, diced
60 ml (4 tbsp) oil
1 egg
few drops vanilla essence or 5 ml (1 tsp) grated orange rind
125 g (4 oz) self-raising flour
150 g (5 oz) caster sugar
1.25 ml (¼ tsp) salt
30 g (1 oz) untoasted wheat germ
30 g (1 oz) desiccated coconut
90 g (3 oz) seedless raisins or sultanas
125 g (4 oz) muesli

Put into bowl in above order and use an electric beater to beat very well until butter has dissolved and mixture can be kneaded into a ball with the hands. Pinch off pieces slightly larger than a walnut, arrange on oiled baking trays and press down with the tines of a fork. Bake on middle shelf of oven at 180°C (350°F, gas 4) for about 20 minutes until lightly browned. Use a spatula to remove to a wire rack to cool and crisp.
Makes about 30 large cookies

BRAN FLAKE CRISPS

125 g (4 oz) soft butter
200 g (7 oz) caster sugar
125 g (4 oz) white bread flour
5 ml (1 tsp) baking powder
pinch of salt
2.5 ml (½ tsp) bicarbonate of soda
5 ml (1 tsp) ground mixed spice
1 egg
few drops vanilla essence
45 g (1½ oz) bran flakes
90 g (3 oz) desiccated coconut
90 g (3 oz) rolled oats

Cream butter and sugar until light. Sift flour, baking powder, salt, bicarbonate of soda and spice and add. Mix well, then add egg beaten with vanilla. When combined, stir in coarsely crushed bran flakes, coconut and oats. Roll into small balls and place on oiled baking trays, leaving plenty of room for spreading. Press down with bottom of a glass. Bake at 180°C (350°F, gas 4) for 20 minutes until browned. Cool on a wire rack.
Makes about 40

SPICED PECAN CRISPS

125 g (4 oz) soft butter
200 g (7 oz) demerara sugar
1 egg
few drops vanilla essence
300 g (11 oz) plain flour
2.5 ml (½ tsp) baking powder
1.25 ml (¼ tsp) bicarbonate of soda
5 ml (1 tsp) ground cinnamon
2.5 ml (½ tsp) grated nutmeg
60 g (2 oz) chopped pecan nuts

Cream butter and sugar until fluffy. Beat in egg and vanilla. Sift dry ingredients and add to creamed mixture, combining thoroughly. Lastly stir in pecan nuts. Form into sausages, wrap in grease-proof paper and freeze for about 45 minutes, until firm.

To bake, slice fairly thinly and place on a lightly oiled baking tray. Bake at 180°C (350°F, gas 4) for 12-15 minutes, until pale golden brown. Cool on a wire rack.
Makes about 54

SPICED SULTANA SLICES

The texture of these lies somewhere between a slab cake and a biscuit. Made without either egg yolks or butter, they are baked in flat strips and then cut into diagonal slices.

1 egg white
5 ml (1 tsp) lemon juice
100 g (3½ oz) caster sugar
140 g (4½ oz) golden syrup
125 ml (4 fl oz) oil
375 g (13 oz) plain flour
5 ml (1 tsp) bicarbonate of soda
pinch of salt
5 ml (1 tsp) ground ginger
5 ml (1 tsp) ground mixed spice
2.5 ml (½ tsp) grated nutmeg
150 g (5 oz) sultanas

Whisk the egg white, lemon juice, sugar, syrup and oil thoroughly. Sift the flour, bicarbonate of soda, salt and spices together, and add slowly to the first mixture, while beating. Stir in sultanas and mix to a dough. Roll the dough into four 2.5-cm (1-in) diameter sausages. Place on oiled baking trays and flatten lightly. Bake on the middle shelf of the oven at 180°C (350°F, gas 4) for 18 minutes, or until nicely browned. Cool for a few minutes and then cut diagonally into slices about 2-cm (¾-in) thick. Cool on a wire rack.
Makes about 40

EASTER BISCUITS

These biscuits are perfect for lunch-boxes as they do not crumble.

275 g (10 oz) plain flour
pinch of salt
5 ml (1 tsp) baking powder
5 ml (1 tsp) ground mixed spice
2.5 ml (½ tsp) ground cinnamon
1.25 ml (¼ tsp) grated nutmeg
125 g (4 oz) soft butter
125 g (4 oz) caster sugar
75 g (2½ oz) currants
60 ml (4 tbsp) chopped mixed peel
1 egg, lightly beaten
extra caster sugar

Sift the flour, salt, baking powder and spices. Rub in butter. Stir in sugar, currants and peel. Add the egg, mix to a dough and then shape into a ball. Do not add any liquid, just knead lightly until mixture holds together. Pat out on floured board and then roll gently with a rolling pin to flatten to about 1-cm (½-in) thick. Cut out rounds with a fluted, 6-cm (2½-in) cutter and place on oiled baking trays. Bake at 180°C (350°F, gas 4) for 12-15 minutes until lightly browned. Remove to a wire rack, sprinkle with caster sugar and cool.
Makes 30-34

COCONUT SLICES

Once chilled, the biscuit dough is sliced into cookies in seconds, making refrigerator biscuits the quickest and easiest to prepare for the oven.

150 g (5 oz) soft butter
200 g (7 oz) caster sugar
1 egg
few drops vanilla essence
250 g (9 oz) plain flour (half brown bread flour may be used)
pinch of salt
2.5 ml (½ tsp) bicarbonate of soda
90 g (3 oz) desiccated coconut.

Cream butter and sugar until light. Add egg and vanilla and beat well. Sift flour with salt and bicarbonate of soda and mix into creamed mixture. Add coconut. Work into a ball and then divide into two 3-cm (1¼-in) diameter sausages. Wrap in greaseproof paper and chill for 1 hour. Using a sharp knife, cut into 5-mm (¼-in) slices and place fairly far apart on an ungreased baking tray. Bake at 160°C (325°F, gas 3) on middle shelf of oven for about 12 minutes. Cool on a wire rack.
Makes about 60

MOCHA CHOCOLATE LOGS

Dipped into melted chocolate and rolled in nuts, these are attractive little logs with the texture of shortbread.

20 ml (4 tsp) instant coffee granules
20 ml (4 tsp) water
250 g (9 oz) soft butter
100 g (3½ oz) caster sugar
few drops vanilla essence
300 g (11 oz) plain flour
60 g (2 oz) cornflour
pinch of salt
plain chocolate and finely chopped almonds

Dissolve coffee granules in water. Add to butter and sugar and cream until light. Add the vanilla. Sift flour, cornflour and salt, add to creamed mixture and beat to a soft dough – a hand-held electric beater may be used. Using a piping bag with a star-shaped nozzle, pipe 5-cm (2-in) long logs on to ungreased baking trays. Bake at 160°C (325°F, gas 3) for 15-20 minutes until a pale golden brown. Stand on trays for a few minutes before removing to a wire rack to cool. Melt the chocolate in a small pan over hot water. Dip one end of each biscuit into the melted chocolate and then roll in nuts until coated. Return to the wire rack for the chocolate to set.
Makes about 48

CINNAMON JAM BISCUITS

Quick to make and economical.

125 g (4 oz) soft butter
150 g (5 oz) demerara sugar
1 egg, lightly beaten
125 g (4 oz) white bread flour
5 ml (1 tsp) bicarbonate of soda
pinch of salt
10 ml (2 tsp) ground cinnamon
45 ml (3 tbsp) smooth apricot jam
125 g (4 oz) wholewheat flour

Cream butter and sugar. Add egg and beat well. Sift white bread flour, bicarbonate of soda, salt and cinnamon and add to creamed mixture together with the jam. Mix well and then add whole-wheat flour and combine to make a soft dough. Push little mounds off the tip of a teaspoon on to oiled baking trays, leaving room for spreading, and bake at 180°C (350°F, gas 4) for 10 minutes or until lightly browned. Cool on a wire rack. Store in airtight container, with a sprinkling of sugar between the layers.
Makes about 40

SNICKERDOODLES

Soft and spicy.

250 g (9 oz) soft butter
200 g (7 oz) caster sugar
2 eggs, lightly beaten
few drops vanilla essence
375 g (13 oz) white bread flour
75 ml (5 tbsp) cornflour
10 ml (2 tsp) cream of tartar
5 ml (1 tsp) bicarbonate of soda
pinch of salt
45 ml (3 tbsp) caster sugar
10 ml (2 tsp) ground cinnamon
2.5 ml (½ tsp) ground mixed spice

Cream butter and sugar. Add eggs and vanilla and beat until creamy. Sift flour, cornflour, cream of tartar, bicarbonate of soda and salt. Add to creamed mixture and mix to a soft dough. Pinch off walnut-sized pieces and roll into small balls. On a large plate mix caster sugar with spices. Roll each ball in this mixture, coating well, then place well apart on ungreased baking tray. Sprinkle any leftover sugar mixture over the tops, and press down lightly with back of fork. Bake at 180°C (350°F, gas 4) for 15 minutes. Initially they will rise like top hats and then settle into disc shapes. Cool on a wire rack.
Makes about 48

GRANNY'S GINGER SNAPS

300 g (11 oz) plain flour
200 g (7 oz) caster sugar
2.5 ml (½ tsp) bicarbonate of soda
2.5 ml (½ tsp) ground mixed spice
pinch of salt
10 ml (2 tsp) ground ginger
125 g (4 oz) soft butter
1 egg
25 ml (5 tsp) thin honey
slivers of preserved ginger

Sift dry ingredients together. Rub in butter. Beat egg and honey and mix into dough, then knead into a ball. Do not add any liquid. Pinch off walnut-sized pieces of dough, roll into balls and place on non-stick or oiled baking tray, with room to spread. Press a sliver of preserved ginger into each, and bake at 160°C (325°F, gas 3) for 20 minutes or until lightly browned. Cool on a wire rack and store in airtight container.
Makes 30-36

FRUITY FRIDGE SQUARES

250 g (9 oz) butter
500 g (18 oz) icing sugar
2 eggs, beaten
200 g (7 oz) Marie biscuits, coarsely broken
90 g (3 oz) desiccated coconut
few drops vanilla essence
75 g (2½ oz) mixed peel
75 g (2½ oz) sultanas

Melt butter over low heat. Slowly blend in sifted icing sugar. Keeping heat very low, stir in eggs – on no account must the mixture boil or they will scramble. Add biscuits. Mix well, remove from hob and add remaining ingredients. Combine thoroughly, using a wooden spoon. Press flat into a shallow dish greased with soft margarine. Cool, and then chill before cutting into small squares. Store in the refrigerator.
Makes about 48

FROM THE TOP: *Mocha Chocolate Logs; Cinnamon Jam Biscuits; Fruity Fridge Squares; Granny's Ginger Snaps.*

OLD-FASHIONED JAM SQUARES

A biscuit base spread with jam and a crumble topping – this recipe fills a large baking tray and is easily made using an electric beater.

250 g (9 oz) soft butter
200 g (7 oz) caster sugar
2 eggs
few drops vanilla essence
500 g (18 oz) plain flour
15 ml (1 tbsp) baking powder
generous pinch of salt
smooth apricot jam
icing sugar

Cream butter and sugar well. Beat eggs with vanilla, add, and mix well. Sift flour, baking powder and salt, beat into creamed mixture and mix well until mixture forms a soft ball that holds together. Pinch off two-thirds of dough and press and pat out evenly into lightly oiled 37 x 25-cm (15 x 10-in) baking tray. Spread generously with jam. Using the coarse side of a grater, grate remaining dough over the top – don't press down, simply spread with a fork. (There is no need to chill the dough first. It should not stick if you run the grater under the tap now and then.) Bake on middle shelf of oven at 180°C (350°F, gas 4) for about 35 minutes until golden brown. Cut into squares and leave to cool in tin. Sift a little icing sugar over the squares before removing.
Makes about 32

BROWN SUGAR COOKIES

Crisp, buttery cookies Granny used to make to fill the biscuit tin.

250 g (9 oz) soft butter
200 g (7 oz) demerara sugar
1 egg, lightly beaten
few drops vanilla essence
375 g (13 oz) self-raising flour
pinch of salt
quartered pecan nuts or
glacé cherries (optional)

Old-fashioned Jam Squares; Coconut Macaroons; Coconut Cherry Stars; Almond Crescents, studded with cloves.

Using an electric beater, cream butter and sugar until light. Add egg and vanilla and beat. Add flour and salt and continue beating until very well combined, then shape into a smooth ball. Pinch off small pieces and roll into balls the size of a large marble. Place on ungreased baking trays and press down with a fork in a criss-cross pattern. If using, gently press a quartered pecan nut or cherry into the top of each. Bake at 180°C (350°F, gas 4) for 15 minutes. Remove to wire racks to cool.
Makes about 48

ALMOND CRESCENTS

These Kourabiedes are the national cookies of Greece, served at weddings, birthday celebrations and christenings. Because they are similar to shortbread in texture, they should be handled delicately.

250 g (9 oz) soft butter, preferably unsalted
100 g (3½ oz) caster sugar
1 egg yolk
15 ml (1 tbsp) brandy
325 g (12 oz) plain flour
45 g (1½ oz) cornflour
75 g (2½ oz) finely chopped, toasted almonds
whole cloves
sifted icing sugar

Cream butter and sugar until pale and fluffy. Add yolk beaten with brandy and beat until combined. Sift flour with cornflour and beat in gradually. Add almonds and knead until smooth. Pinch off small pieces and shape into crescents. Place on ungreased baking trays and insert a clove into the top of each. Bake at 150°C (300°F, gas 2) for about 30 minutes. Test by cutting one in half – there should be no trace of a buttery streak. Carefully roll the crescents, while still warm, in icing sugar. Place on wire racks and sift more icing sugar over the crescents – they should be well coated. Leave until cold before storing in airtight container.
Makes about 48

COCONUT CHERRY STARS

Bright, dainty little morsels.

125 g (4 oz) very soft butter
45 ml (3 tbsp) sifted icing sugar
100 g (3½ oz) plain flour
25 ml (5 tsp) cornflour
few drops vanilla essence
75 ml (5 tbsp) desiccated coconut
12 glacé cherries, halved
25 ml (5 tsp) water (optional)

Cream butter and icing sugar. Sift flour and cornflour, add to creamed mixture and beat well. Add vanilla and coconut. Mix well, adding up to 25 ml (5 tsp) water if dough is too stiff. Using a piping bag fitted with a star-shaped nozzle, pipe on to ungreased baking trays. Press half a cherry into each and bake at 160°C (325°F, gas 3) for 20 minutes until pale gold. Cool on a wirerack.
Makes 16-24

> **NOTE**
> * It is important to use soft butter, extra large eggs, and an electric beater, otherwise the mixture will not bind sufficiently.*

SPICED COFFEE DROPS

Disc-shaped, soft and spicy.

250 g (9 oz) soft butter
400 g (14 oz) demerara sugar
2 eggs
15 ml (1 tbsp) instant coffee granules
125 ml (4 fl oz) cold water
500 g (18 oz) white bread flour plus 10 ml (2 tsp) extra
5 ml (1 tsp) bicarbonate of soda
1.25 ml (¼ tsp) salt
5 ml (1 tsp) ground cinnamon
2.5 ml (½ tsp) grated nutmeg
large pinch of ground cloves
chocolate chips (optional)

Cream butter and sugar. Beat in eggs, one at a time. Dissolve coffee in water and add together with the 10 ml (2 tsp) flour. Beat well. Sift flour, bicarbonate of soda, salt and spices. Mix into creamed mixture to make a soft dough. Chill for at least 1 hour. Using a teaspoon, push mounds of dough off on to oiled baking trays, leaving plenty of room for spreading. Press a chocolate chip lightly into the top of each, or leave plain. Bake at 180°C (350°F, gas 4) for 13-15 minutes, until golden brown. Using a spatula, remove to a wire rack to cool. Store in airtight container, with a sprinkling of sugar between layers.
Makes about 80

MUESLI BARS

125 g (4 oz) soft butter
200 g (7 oz) demerara sugar
1 egg, beaten
125 g (4 oz) wholewheat flour
45 g (1½ oz) rolled oats
125 g (4 oz) muesli
30 g (1 oz) desiccated coconut
75 g (2½ oz) sultanas
5 ml (1 tsp) baking powder
5 ml (1 tsp) ground cinnamon
2.5 ml (½ tsp) ground mixed spice
60 g (2 oz) chopped nuts or
75 ml (5 tbsp) sunflower seeds

Cream butter and sugar. Add egg and beat well. Add rest of ingredients and mix to a soft dough – use an electric beater. The mixture will seem rather crumbly, but it binds together as you press it out. Press into a lightly oiled, 33 x 20-cm (13 x 8-in) Swiss roll tin, and bake at 180°C (350°F, gas 4) for 20 minutes. Cut into bars – they will be very soft, but will crisp on cooling. Cool in tin, remove carefully to a wire rack and leave until cold.
Makes about 24

COCONUT MACAROONS

1 egg
100 g (3½ oz) caster sugar
few drops vanilla essence
pinch of salt
180 g (6 oz) desiccated coconut
quartered glacé cherries or halved almonds

Beat egg, sugar, vanilla and salt until very light and creamy. Gradually beat in coconut to make a moist and crumbly mixture. Using a teaspoon, push small mounds on to an oiled baking tray which has been dusted with cornflour. Pinch with fingers into pyramids. Top the macaroons with cherries or almonds. Bake at 150°C (300°F, gas 2) for 20 minutes or until just beginning to brown. Gently loosen with spatula and remove to a wire rack to cool.
Makes about 20

CHOCOLATE CRINKLES

The ultimate crunchy sandwiched biscuits, filled with melted chocolate.

125 g (4 oz) soft butter
100 g (3½ oz) caster sugar
75 g (2½ oz) self-raising flour
pinch of salt
75 g (2½ oz) wholewheat flour
60 g (2 oz) desiccated coconut
few drops vanilla essence
25 ml (5 tsp) cocoa powder
30 ml (2 tbsp) boiling water
melted plain or milk chocolate

Cream butter and sugar. Add self-raising flour sifted with salt. When well mixed add wholewheat flour, coconut and vanilla. Mix well, then stir in cocoa creamed with boiling water. Beat into flour mixture to make a soft dough. Gather into a ball and pinch off small pieces the size of large marbles. Place on oiled baking trays. Press down heavily with fork to score deeply. Bake at 180°C (350°F, gas 4) for 15 minutes. Cool on a wire rack, and when cold sandwich together with melted chocolate.
Makes about 22 sandwiches

RAISIN OAT BARS

60 g (2 oz) soft butter
60 ml (4 tbsp) demerara sugar
45 ml (3 tbsp) golden syrup
2 eggs, lightly beaten
60 g (2 oz) plain flour
7.5 ml (1½ tsp) baking powder
5 ml (1 tsp) ground mixed spice
60 g (2 oz) wholewheat flour
125 g (4 oz) seedless raisins
45 g (1½ oz) rolled oats
icing sugar (optional)

Cream butter and sugar. Add syrup and eggs and beat well. Sift plain flour, baking powder and spice and mix into creamed mixture. Mix in wholewheat flour, raisins and oats. Combine well – the mixture will be soft and sticky. Turn into an oiled 23-cm (9-in) square baking tin and spread evenly, using a dampened spoon or rubber spatula. Bake at 180°C (350°F, gas 4) for 25 minutes, until browned, risen and firm. Cut into bars and cool in tin. Leave plain, or, before removing, sift a little icing sugar on top. Store in airtight container.
Makes about 18 large bars

FRUITY OAT CRISPS

125 g (4 oz) soft butter
100 g (3½ oz) demerara sugar
few drops vanilla essence
60 g (2 oz) plain flour
150 g (5 oz) rolled oats
125 g (4 oz) mixed dried fruit
pinch of salt
2.5 ml (½ tsp) bicarbonate of soda
10 ml (2 tsp) hot water

Cream butter, sugar and vanilla. Add flour, oats, fruit and salt. Mix well, then beat in bicarbonate of soda dissolved in hot water. Mix to a soft dough, pinch off small pieces and roll into balls, flouring your palms occasionally if necessary. Place on oiled baking trays and press down lightly with a fork. Bake at 180°C (350°F, gas 4) for 15 minutes. Leave to crisp on trays for a few minutes before removing to a wire rack to cool.
Makes about 28

PEANUT BUTTER BISCUITS

45 ml (3 tbsp) peanut butter
125 g (4 oz) soft butter
few drops vanilla essence
150 g (5 oz) demerara sugar
1 egg, lightly beaten
125 g (4 oz) white bread flour plus
5 ml (1 tsp) extra
pinch of salt
2.5 ml (½ tsp) bicarbonate of soda
125 g (4 oz) brown bread flour

Cream peanut butter, butter and vanilla. Beat in sugar very well or it will not dissolve. Add egg plus 5 ml (1 tsp) extra flour and beat well. Sift in white bread flour, salt and bicarbonate of soda. Finally mix in brown bread flour and knead until dough holds together. Roll small pieces into balls and place on oiled baking trays, leaving room for spreading. Flatten with a wet fork in a criss-cross pattern, and bake at 180°C (350°F, gas 4) for 20 minutes. Cool on a wire rack.
Makes about 36

Crisp Chocolate Crinkles and elegant Vanilla Viennese Twirls.

SPICED COCONUT BISCUITS

A simple, crunchy cookie with spices adding a lovely zip to the flavour.

125 g (4 oz) soft butter
150 g (5 oz) caster sugar
1 egg
few drops vanilla essence
250 g (9 oz) self-raising flour
pinch of salt
5 ml (1 tsp) ground cinnamon
1.25 ml (¼ tsp) grated nutmeg
75 g (2½ oz) desiccated coconut
pecan nuts, halved (optional)

Cream butter and sugar until light. Beat egg with vanilla and add, mixing well. Sift flour, salt and spices and add, then finally mix in coconut and combine thoroughly. Knead into a ball with your hands, then pinch off small pieces and roll into balls. Place on oiled baking trays, allowing for spreading, and press flat with a fork, or press half a pecan nut into the top of each. Bake at 180°C (350°F, gas 4) for 15-18 minutes until a deep beige colour. Cool on a wire rack.
Makes about 36

CRUNCHIES

A super version of this old favourite; it is designed to fill the average 37 x 25-cm (15 x 10-in) baking tray to the brim, requires slightly less butter and sugar than usual, and is made extra nutritious with the addition of raisins and/or sunflower seeds.

250 g (9 oz) rolled oats
300 g (11 oz) demerara sugar
125 g (4 oz) brown bread flour
60 g (2 oz) plain flour
100 g (3½ oz) desiccated coconut
90 g (3 oz) seedless raisins
60 g (2 oz) sunflower seeds
250 g (9 oz) butter
45 ml (3 tbsp) honey
10 ml (2 tsp) bicarbonate of soda

Mix oats, sugar, flours, coconut, raisins and sunflower seeds. Melt butter and honey together over low heat – the mixture will brown slowly and this adds to the flavour. Stir in bicarbonate of soda and when mixture froths, add to dry ingredients, mix well and press firmly into an oiled, 37 x 25-cm (15 x 10-in) baking tray. Bake on middle shelf of oven at 180°C (350°F, gas 4) for 18-20 minutes until richly browned. Cut into jumbo bars and remove when cold.
Makes about 30 jumbo bars

VANILLA VIENNESE TWIRLS

Melt-in-the-mouth little shortbreads, sandwiched with vanilla butter icing.

250 g (9 oz) soft butter
45 g (1½ oz) sifted icing sugar
250 g (9 oz) plain flour
45 ml (3 tbsp) cornflour
few drops vanilla essence

ICING
60 g (2 oz) sifted icing sugar
30 g (1 oz) soft butter
few drops vanilla essence

Cream butter and sugar. Sift flour and cornflour. Add to creamed mixture together with vanilla and mix well to a soft dough. Pipe rosettes on to ungreased baking trays and bake at 160°C (325°F, gas 3) for 20 minutes until pale gold. Cool on a wire rack.

Beat ingredients for icing together until smooth. Use to sandwich biscuits.
Makes about 24 single biscuits

CHOCOLATE LOGS

250 g (9 oz) soft butter
60 g (2 oz) sifted icing sugar
few drops vanilla essence
15 ml (1 tbsp) cocoa powder
200 g (7 oz) plain flour
45 g (1½ oz) cornflour
pinch of salt

VANILLA BUTTER ICING
60 g (2 oz) sifted icing sugar
nut of soft butter
few drops vanilla essence
5 ml (1 tsp) milk
chocolate vermicelli

Cream butter, icing sugar and vanilla until light. Sift cocoa, flour, cornflour and salt and add to creamed mixture. Mix to a soft dough and fill piping bag fitted with a fluted nozzle. Pipe into 7.5-cm (3-in) long logs on to ungreased baking trays. Bake at 160°C (325°F, gas 3) for 30 minutes, then cool on a wire rack.

To make icing, combine all ingredients, except vermicelli, until creamy. Spread over tops of logs and sprinkle with vermicelli.
Makes about 36

NOTE
● *If preferred, the icing may be omitted, in which case simply brush the unbaked logs with lightly beaten egg white, sprinkle with chocolate vermicelli and bake as above.*

CHOCOLATE CHIP BISCUITS

Large, crisp cookies studded with nuts and chocolate chips which do not melt in the baking.

125 g (4 oz) soft butter
75 g (2½ oz) caster sugar
60 ml (4 tbsp) demerara sugar
1 egg
few drops vanilla essence
150 g (5 oz) plain flour
45 ml (3 tbsp) cornflour
2.5 ml (½ tsp) bicarbonate of soda
pinch of salt
60 g (2 oz) chopped walnuts
or pecan nuts
125 g (4 oz) chocolate chips

Cream butter with both sugars. Beat egg with vanilla and add, mixing well. Sift flour, cornflour, bicarbonate of soda and salt together. Add to creamed mixture, mixing to a soft dough. Stir in nuts and chocolate chips. Shape dough into a ball, pinch off pieces and roll into balls, flouring your palms occasionally if necessary. Place on oiled baking trays, leaving room for spreading, and flatten lightly with a fork. Bake at 180°C (350°F, gas 4) for 15 minutes. Carefully remove to a wire rack to cool.
Makes about 40

FRUIT OAT SQUARES

These biscuits keep well and are similar to crunchies, except that they're softer and bursting with fruit and other wholesome ingredients.

250 g (9 oz) mixed dried fruit
250 g (9 oz) butter
30 ml (2 tbsp) honey
225 g (8 oz) rolled oats
125 g (4 oz) wholewheat flour
125 g (4 oz) white bread flour
30 g (1 oz) wheat germ
90 g (3 oz) desiccated coconut
150 g (5 oz) demerara sugar
10 ml (2 tsp) ground mixed spice
10 ml (2 tsp) bicarbonate of soda

Put fruit, butter and honey into heavy-based saucepan and bring to a slow boil, stirring to melt the butter. Mix oats, flours, wheat germ, coconut, sugar and spice in large bowl. Add bicarbonate of soda to hot mixture, stirring vigorously, and when mixture froths, stir into dry ingredients. Mix well and then press into an oiled, 37 x 25-cm (15 x 10-in) baking tray. Pat in firmly and evenly, and bake on middle shelf of oven at 180°C (350°F, gas 4) for 15-20 minutes until browned. Cut into squares and leave in tin until cold.
Makes about 35

> NOTE
> ● *It is important to use soft butter, extra large eggs, and an electric beater, otherwise the butter might not 'melt' sufficiently to bind the mixture.*

LEMON SULTANA SNAPS

These super biscuits spread into very crisp, golden-brown rounds.

125 g (4 oz) soft butter
few drops vanilla essence
finely grated rind of 1 lemon
100 g (3½ oz) caster sugar
60 g (2 oz) plain flour
pinch of salt
2.5 ml (½ tsp) bicarbonate of soda
60 g (2 oz) wholewheat flour
75 g (2½ oz) sultanas

Cream butter with vanilla, lemon rind and sugar until light. Sift plain flour with salt and bicarbonate of soda, add to creamed mixture and mix. Add wholewheat flour and when combined, add sultanas. Mix well, then knead into a ball. Pinch off small pieces, roll into balls, and place on oiled baking trays, leaving room for spreading. Flatten two ways, making a criss-cross pattern, with a fork dipped into water. Bake at 180°C (350°F, gas 4) for 15 minutes. Stand for 1 minute to crisp, then use a spatula to remove to a wire rack to cool.
Makes about 28

WHOLEWHEAT AND OAT GINGER CRISPS

Thin, crunchy, economical cookies.

250 g (9 oz) soft butter
200 g (7 oz) demerara sugar
125 g (4 oz) wholewheat flour
275 g (10 oz) rolled oats
15 ml (1 tbsp) ground ginger
1.25 ml (¼ tsp) salt
few drops vanilla essence
2.5 ml (½ tsp) bicarbonate of soda
45 ml (3 tbsp) boiling water

Cream butter and sugar until light. Add flour, oats, ginger, salt and vanilla. Mix well. Add bicarbonate of soda dissolved in boiling water. Combine thoroughly, then work into a soft ball. Place tea-spoonfuls of dough on an oiled baking tray, leaving room for spreading. Bake at 180°C (350°F, gas 4) for about 15 minutes until lightly browned and spread into flat rounds. Leave on tray for a minute to crisp, then remove with spatula to a wire rack to cool.
Makes about 48

ORANGE BISCUIT PRESS COOKIES

Delicately flavoured, with a short texture. Serve plain, or sandwich with orange-flavoured butter icing.

125 g (4 oz) soft butter
45 ml (3 tbsp) caster sugar
finely grated rind of ½ orange
125 g (4 oz) plain flour
45 ml (3 tbsp) cornflour
45 g (1½ oz) desiccated coconut

Cream butter, sugar and rind until very light. Mix in flour sifted with cornflour. Add coconut and then beat well until mixture forms a ball. Using a biscuit press, press into desired shapes on to ungreased baking trays. Bake at 160°C (325°F, gas 3) for 20 minutes. Cool on a wire rack.
Makes about 24

FROM THE TOP: *Fruit Oat Squares; Lemon Sultana Snaps; Orange Biscuit Press Cookies; Chocolate Chip Biscuits.*

SIMPLE COCOA CRISPS

Economical and very quick to make.

100 g (3½ oz) demerara sugar
100 g (3½ oz) caster sugar
125 ml (4 fl oz) oil
1 egg, beaten
45 g (1½ oz) desiccated coconut
few drops vanilla essence
pinch of salt
2.5 ml (½ tsp) bicarbonate of soda
60 g (2 oz) brown bread flour
175 g (6 oz) rolled oats
25 ml (5 tsp) cocoa powder

Put ingredients into bowl in above order and beat until well mixed – the mixture will be crumbly. Press together into a ball with your hands, then scoop up teaspoonfuls and place on oiled baking trays, leaving plenty of room for spreading. Pinch into little pyramids with your fingers. Bake at 180°C (350°F, gas 4) for 20 minutes. Leave on trays to crisp for 1 minute before removing with spatula to a wire rack to cool.
Makes about 28

OAT, SULTANA AND COCONUT BARS

60 g (2 oz) butter
60 ml (4 tbsp) oil
90 g (3 oz) rolled oats
75 g (2½ oz) sultanas
125 g (4 oz) self-raising flour
100 g (3½ oz) caster sugar
45 g (1½ oz) desiccated coconut
few drops vanilla essence

Place butter and oil in a small heavy-based saucepan and heat gently just until butter melts. Mix remaining ingredients and stir in melted shortening. Using an electric beater, mix well to a soft, crumbly consistency. Press firmly into an oiled 23-cm (9-in) square baking tin. Bake on middle shelf of oven at 180°C (350°F, gas 4) for 25 minutes, until just beginning to colour. Cut into bars and leave in tin until cold.
Makes about 18

Simple Cocoa Crisps; Orange Liqueur Wafers; Quick Date and Nut Bars.

WALNUT FRIDGE CRISPS

Delicious, crisp cookies.

250 g (9 oz) plain flour
5 ml (1 tsp) baking powder
pinch of salt
2.5 ml (½ tsp) bicarbonate of soda
5 ml (1 tsp) ground mixed spice
125 g (4 oz) butter
100 g (3½ oz) demerara sugar
100 g (3½ oz) caster sugar
1 egg
few drops vanilla essence
60 g (2 oz) finely chopped walnuts

Sift the flour, baking powder, salt, bicarbonate of soda and mixed spice together. Cream the butter and slowly add the brown and white sugars, beating well. Beat the egg and vanilla together and add to butter mixture, then mix in the flour mixture — an electric beater is perfect for the job. Lastly add walnuts. Form the dough into two long sausages, wrap in greaseproof paper and chill until firm enough to slice. Cut into thin rounds and bake on an ungreased baking tray at 180°C (350°F, gas 4) for about 15 minutes. Cool on a wire rack.
Makes about 54

CARROT, DATE AND SUNFLOWER SEED BISCUITS

Big, flat, quick-mix cookies.

100 g (3½ oz) demerara sugar
100 g (3½ oz) caster sugar
125 g (4 oz) soft butter
1 egg, beaten
90 g (3 oz) coarsely grated carrots
5 ml (1 tsp) ground cinnamon
1.25 ml (¼ tsp) grated nutmeg
pinch of salt
2.5 ml (½ tsp) bicarbonate of soda
60 g (2 oz) brown bread flour
175 g (6 oz) rolled oats
125 g (4 oz) stoned dates, finely chopped
60 g (2 oz) sunflower seeds, preferably toasted

Beat all ingredients, except sunflower seeds, until very well combined. Add sunflower seeds and mix to a soft dough. Scoop up teaspoonfuls and push off on to oiled baking trays, leaving plenty of room for spreading. Bake at 180°C (350°F, gas 4) for 15 minutes, then allow to crisp on trays for about 1 minute before carefully removing, using a spatula, to a wire rack to cool.
Makes about 40

CHINESE CHEWS

These soft bars firm up with storing and develop a gingery flavour.

125 g (4 oz) soft butter
150 g (5 oz) demerara sugar
2 eggs
125 g (4 oz) white bread flour
5 ml (1 tsp) baking powder
60 g (2 oz) chopped walnuts or pecan nuts
125 g (4 oz) stoned dates, chopped
60 g (2 oz) chopped glacé cherries
2 large knobs preserved ginger, chopped
few drops vanilla essence
caster sugar

Cream butter and sugar. Add eggs one by one, beating well. Sift flour and baking powder, add nuts and fruit and toss to mix. Stir into creamed mixture, add vanilla and mix well to a thick batter. Turn into an oiled, 25 x 20-cm (10 x 8-in) baking tin, spreading evenly, and bake at 180°C (350°F, gas 4) for 25 minutes or until light brown and firm. Dust with a little caster sugar, cut into bars and leave in tin until cold.
Makes about 24

ORANGE LIQUEUR WAFERS

Light, melt-in-the-mouth little slices, to serve with sorbets or ice cream.

125 g (4 oz) soft butter
100 g (3½ oz) caster sugar
25 ml (5 tsp) orange-flavoured liqueur
125 g (4 oz) plain flour
45 ml (3 tbsp) cornflour
pinch of salt
5 ml (1 tsp) finely grated orange rind
extra caster sugar

Cream butter, sugar and liqueur until fluffy. Sift flour, cornflour and salt and blend into butter mixture. Mix in orange rind and shape into a ball, then roll into a long, smooth sausage. Wrap in greaseproof paper and chill for about 1 hour. Slice thinly, using a sharp knife, and arrange on an ungreased baking tray, leaving room for spreading. Bake at 180°C (350°F, gas 4) for 10 minutes, or until pale gold. Dust with caster sugar and leave on baking tray to cool slightly, then lift carefully on to wire racks to cool completely.
Makes 42-48

QUICK DATE AND NUT BARS

250 g (9 oz) stoned dates, chopped
2 eggs, lightly beaten
75 g (2½ oz) demerara sugar
60 ml (4 tbsp) oil
60 g (2 oz) wholewheat flour
45 g (1½ oz) rolled oats
5 ml (1 tsp) baking powder
5 ml (1 tsp) ground mixed spice
pinch of salt
60 g (2 oz) chopped walnuts or pecan nuts
few drops vanilla essence
icing sugar

Mix all ingredients, except icing sugar, in the order given. Spoon evenly into an oiled, 23-cm (9-in) square baking tin and bake at 180°C (350°F, gas 4) for 25 minutes, until brown and firm. Cut into bars and cool in tin. Dust with icing sugar when cold.
Makes about 18 large bars

MUESLI MUNCHIES

60 g (2 oz) plain flour
5 ml (1 tsp) cream of tartar
2.5 ml (½ tsp) bicarbonate of soda
pinch of salt
5 ml (1 tsp) ground mixed spice
125 g (4 oz) wholewheat flour
150 g (5 oz) demerara sugar
150 ml (¼ pint) oil
2 eggs
90 g (3 oz) muesli
60 g (2 oz) sultanas
45 g (1½ oz) desiccated coconut

Sift dry ingredients. Add wholewheat flour. Whisk together sugar, oil and eggs. Add to dry ingredients together with muesli, sultanas and coconut. Mix very well to a soft dough. Push large teaspoonfuls off on to oiled baking trays, with plenty of room to spread. Flatten lightly with tines of a fork dipped into water. Bake at 180°C (350°F, gas 4) for 18 minutes. Using a spatula, transfer to wire racks to cool.
Makes about 30

SUNFLOWER SEED AND HONEY COOKIES

90 g (3 oz) rolled oats
125 g (4 oz) white bread flour
100 g (3½ oz) caster sugar
45 g (1½ oz) desiccated coconut
75 g (2½ oz) currants, plumped in hot water
60 g (2 oz) sunflower seeds, preferably toasted
60 g (2 oz) butter
60 ml (4 tbsp) oil
30 ml (2 tbsp) honey
2.5 ml (½ tsp) bicarbonate of soda
15 ml (1 tbsp) hot water
1 egg, beaten
few drops vanilla essence

Mix oats, flour, sugar, coconut, drained currants and sunflower seeds. Heat butter, oil and honey in a small heavy-based saucepan until just melted. Dissolve bicarbonate of soda in hot water and add to melted mixture. Stir foaming mixture into dry ingredients. Mix well to a crumbly dough – using an electric beater – then add egg and vanilla and continue beating until mixture forms a soft ball. Push teaspoonfuls of mixture off on to lightly oiled baking trays, leaving room to spread, and bake on middle shelf of oven at 180°C (350°F, gas 4) for 15 minutes or until browned and firm. Cool on wire racks.
Makes about 28

ORANGE AND OAT MACAROONS

200 g (7 oz) demerara sugar
200 g (7 oz) caster sugar
250 ml (8 fl oz) oil
2 eggs, beaten
90 g (3 oz) desiccated coconut
few drops vanilla essence
1.25 ml (¼ tsp) salt
5 ml (1 tsp) bicarbonate of soda
10 ml (2 tsp) finely grated orange rind
60 g (2 oz) chopped mixed peel
125 g (4 oz) white bread flour
375 g (13 oz) rolled oats

Place ingredients in a large bowl in the order given. Mix well, then shape into a soft ball. The dough will be loose and slippery. Place teaspoonfuls on oiled baking trays, pinching gently to shape and leaving plenty of room for spreading. Bake at 180°C (350°F, gas 4) for 15 minutes. Stand for 1 minute to crisp. Use a spatula to remove to a wire rack to cool. Store in airtight container, with sugar sprinkled between each layer.
Makes about 80

SPICED MINCEMEAT BARS

BASE
500 g (18 oz) plain flour
15 ml (1 tbsp) baking powder
1.25 ml (¼ tsp) salt
10 ml (2 tsp) ground cinnamon
5 ml (1 tsp) ground mixed spice
200 g (7 oz) icing sugar
250 g (9 oz) soft butter
2 eggs, beaten

FILLING
450 g (1 lb) fruit mincemeat
1 large Granny Smith apple, peeled and coarsely grated
25ml (5 tsp) brandy
extra icing sugar

Sift dry ingredients. Rub in the butter, and then add eggs. (An electric mixer may be used.) Knead to a ball, wrap and freeze until firm, about 45 minutes. Remove three-quarters of the dough from the freezer and grate coarsely into a large, lightly oiled square or rectangular baking tin. Pat down with your hands to form a smooth, 5-mm (¼-in) thick base.

For the filling, mix fruit mincemeat, apple and brandy, and spread evenly over dough. Remove remaining dough from freezer and grate coarsely over the top, spreading evenly with a fork. Bake at 160°C (325°F, gas 3) for 50 minutes or until crisp. Cut into bars and cool in tin. Dust with icing sugar, remove and place on a wire rack until completely cold.
Makes about 40

HONEYED SEED COOKIES

Intriguing, caramel-coloured biscuits, containing sunflower seeds and wholewheat flour. The crisp sesame topping makes them singularly attractive cookies.

125 g (4 oz) soft butter
few drops vanilla essence
100 g (3½ oz) demerara sugar
25 ml (5 tsp) honey
75 g (2½ oz) plain flour
pinch of salt
2.5 ml (½ tsp) bicarbonate of soda
75 g (2½ oz) wholewheat flour
45 g (1½ oz) sunflower seeds, preferably lightly toasted
about 45 ml (3 tbsp) sesame seeds

Cream butter, vanilla, sugar and honey. Sift plain flour with salt and bicarbonate of soda, and mix in. Add wholewheat flour and sunflower seeds. Beat well to make a soft dough, then shape into a ball. Pinch off small pieces and flatten between your palms. Dip tops in sesame seeds, coating thoroughly. Place on oiled baking trays, allowing room for spreading. Bake at 180°C (350°F, gas 4) for about 12 minutes, until browned. Allow to crisp on trays for 1 minute before removing to a wire rack to cool.
Makes about 26

ORANGE, HONEY AND RAISIN CRISPS

Nutritious brown biscuits made with oil, honey and wholewheat flour.

125 ml (4 fl oz) oil
25 ml (5 tsp) honey
100 g (3½ oz) caster sugar
5 ml (1 tsp) finely grated orange rind
100 g (3½ oz) wholewheat flour
45 g (1½ oz) self-raising flour
pinch of salt
45 g (1½ oz) desiccated coconut
45 g (1½ oz) seedless raisins
1 egg, lightly beaten

Whisk together the oil, honey, sugar and rind. Add flours, salt, coconut and raisins. Mix well, add egg and mix to a soft, rather oily dough. Roll into balls and place on lightly oiled baking trays. Flatten with bottom of a glass. Bake at 180°C (350°F, gas 4) for 15 minutes or until firm and richly browned. Cool on a wire rack.
Makes about 28

CHOCOLATE DIGESTIVES

Serve these wholesome biscuits plain or topped with chocolate.

275 g (10 oz) rolled oats
125 g (4 oz) wholewheat flour
60 g (2 oz) self-raising flour
pinch of salt
60 ml (4 tbsp) caster sugar
125 g (4 oz) butter
45 ml (3 tbsp) honey
about 45 ml (3 tbsp) milk

TOPPING
100 g (3½ oz) plain chocolate
10 ml (2 tsp) water
10 ml (2 tsp) butter

Process oats in a food processor fitted with grinding blade, until fairly fine, but do not grind to a meal. Mix with both flours and salt. Add sugar. Melt butter with honey over low heat – the mixture must just have melted without bubbling. Slowly beat into flour mixture. Mix well, then add just enough milk to make a soft dough. Pat out on to lightly floured board, and roll flat, about 3-mm (⅛-in) thick, with a rolling pin. Using a 6-cm (2½-in) cutter, cut into rounds, place on oiled baking trays and prick each biscuit well with a fork. Bake at 180°C (350°F, gas 4) for 12 minutes – watch carefully, as they brown quickly round the edges. Cool on a wire rack.

To make the topping: break up the chocolate, add the water and butter and melt over low heat. Remove, stir until smooth, then spread the chocolate thinly over the top of each cooled biscuit. Place on a wire rack to set before storing.
Makes about 50

FROM THE TOP: *Chocolate Digestives; Spiced Mincemeat Bars; Orange and Oat Macaroons; Honeyed Seed Cookies.*

Caramel Squares; Featherlight Chocolate Swirls; Iced Chocolate Squares; Clove-studded Spicy Brown Biscuits.

Caramel Squares

The richest, sweetest biscuits.

250 g (9 oz) butter
150 g (5 oz) caster sugar
250 g (9 oz) plain flour
5 ml (1 tsp) baking powder
5 ml (1 tsp) ground cinnamon
45-75 ml (3-5 tbsp) finely chopped
pecan nuts

FILLING
225 g (8 oz) canned condensed milk
25 ml (5 tsp) golden syrup
25 ml (5 tsp) caster sugar
25 ml (5 tsp) water
30 g (1 oz) butter
few drops vanilla essence

Cream butter and sugar. Sift flour with baking powder and cinnamon and add to creamed mixture. Mix well – the dough will be very soft. Press two-thirds of the mixture evenly into a lightly oiled, 33 x 20-cm (13 x 8-in) Swiss roll tin. Add the nuts to the remaining third, wrap in greaseproof paper and place in freezer. Bake the base at 160°C (325°F, gas 3) for 15 minutes.

Meanwhile, make filling by placing condensed milk, syrup, sugar, water and butter in small, heavy-based saucepan. Bring to the boil over low heat, stirring all the time to dissolve the sugar, and then boil gently until thick and a light caramel in colour. Stir continually and take care that it doesn't catch on the bottom as it burns very easily. Remove and add vanilla, then pour over half-baked base, spreading evenly. Grate chilled dough coarsely over the top. Bake on middle shelf of oven at 160°C (325°F, gas 3) for 25 minutes or until the filling is the colour of fudge. Cut into squares and cool in tin before removing.
Makes about 24

HINT
● *When measuring honey or syrup, use a measure which has been oiled, or used to measure oil – the honey or syrup will slide out easily.*

Featherlight Chocolate Swirls

A light and fluffy mixture, resulting in pale, melt-in-the-mouth dainties.

125 g (4 oz) soft butter
100 g (3½ oz) caster sugar
1 egg, lightly beaten
few drops vanilla essence
200 g (7 oz) self-raising flour
45 g (1½ oz) cornflour
45 g (1½ oz) plain chocolate
45 ml (3 tbsp) water
glacé cherries

Cream butter and sugar until light. Beat in egg and vanilla. Sift flour with cornflour and mix in. Place broken up chocolate in small container, add water, and melt over simmering water. Add to the creamed mixture and beat until thoroughly combined. Use an electric beater, and the mixture will soon become the correct consistency for piping. Fill piping bag fitted with a star nozzle and pipe in small whorls on to baking trays lined with waxed paper, leaving room for spreading. Press a quartered cherry into the top of each. Bake at 160°C (325°F, gas 3) for 20 minutes. Using a spatula, remove to a wire rack to cool.
Makes 24-30

Clove-studded Spicy Brown Biscuits

These easy-to-make, economical cookies should be kept for a few days to allow the flavour to develop.

125 g (4 oz) soft butter
150 g (5 oz) caster sugar
1 egg, beaten
45 ml (3 tbsp) golden syrup
375 g (13 oz) white bread flour
5 ml (1 tsp) bicarbonate of soda
1.25 ml (¼ tsp) salt
5 ml (1 tsp) ground cinnamon
10 ml (2 tsp) ground mixed spice
whole cloves

Cream the butter, sugar, egg and syrup together. Sift the flour, bicarbonate of soda, salt and ground spices together and add. Mix into a ball, pinch off pieces, roll into small balls and place on oiled baking trays. Press a clove into the centre of each and bake on middle shelf of oven at 180°C (350°F, gas 4) for 12 minutes, or until lightly browned. Cool on a wire rack.
Makes about 40

Iced Chocolate Squares

A crunchie base spread with a dark, sweet topping.

BASE
100 g (3½ oz) caster sugar
125 g (4 oz) brown bread flour
90 g (3 oz) desiccated coconut
25 ml (5 tsp) cocoa powder
2.5 ml (½ tsp) bicarbonate of soda
90 g (3 oz) rolled oats
125 g (4 oz) soft butter
few drops vanilla essence

TOPPING
175 g (6 oz) sifted icing sugar
10 ml (2 tsp) cocoa powder
small nut of butter
few drops vanilla essence
hot water

In a large bowl mix together the sugar, flour, coconut, cocoa, bicarbonate of soda and oats. Beat in the butter and vanilla until thoroughly combined. Press the mixture firmly into an oiled, 33 x 20-cm (13 x 8-in) Swiss roll tin and bake at 180°C (350°F, gas 4) for 20 minutes. Cut into squares and leave in tin to cool slightly before spreading with topping.

For the topping, beat icing sugar, cocoa, butter and vanilla together, adding just enough hot water to make a spreading consistency – do not use too much or the icing will not set. Spread over base and re-cut squares when set. Remove when cold.
Makes about 30 large squares

FRUIT DROPS

These are economical, spicy and wholesome chews, using oil, dried fruit and wholewheat flour.

125 g (4 oz) plain flour
2.5 ml (½ tsp) baking powder
5 ml (1 tsp) bicarbonate of soda
pinch of salt
5 ml (1 tsp) ground cinnamon
2.5 ml (½ tsp) grated nutmeg
pinch of ground cloves
2 eggs
150 ml (¼ pint) oil
100 g (3½ oz) caster sugar
100 g (3½ oz) demerara sugar
125 g (4 oz) wholewheat flour
90 g (3 oz) rolled oats
45 g (1½ oz) desiccated coconut
275 g (10 oz) mixed dried fruit

Sift plain flour, baking powder, bicarbonate of soda, salt and spices. Beat eggs well with oil and both sugars. Mix into sifted mixture, then add wholewheat flour, oats, coconut and fruit. Mix well. Place teaspoonfuls on well-oiled baking trays, leaving room for spreading. Bake in the centre of the oven at l80°C (350°F, gas 4) for 12-15 minutes until browned. Cool on a wire rack.
Makes about 48

FIVE-STAR FRUIT SQUARES

Richly browned, sweet, cake-like bars.

250 g (9 oz) self-raising flour
5 ml (1 tsp) ground cinnamon
2.5 ml (½ tsp) grated nutmeg
pinch of ground cloves
200 g (7 oz) caster sugar
140 g (4½ oz) desiccated coconut
275 g (10 oz) mixed dried fruit
45 g (1½ oz) toasted sunflower seeds
200 ml (7 fl oz) oil
100 g (3½ oz) butter, melted
2 eggs, beaten
45 g (1½ oz) bran flakes, coarsely crushed
few drops vanilla essence

Sift flour with spices into a large mixing bowl. Using a wooden spoon, mix in remaining ingredients, stirring well to combine. Press mixture very firmly and evenly into an oiled, 25 x 20 x 6-cm (10 x 8 x 2½-in) baking or small roasting tin. Bake on middle shelf of oven at 180°C (350°F, gas 4) for 35 minutes until risen, browned and firm – do not overbake. Cut into squares or bars and leave in tin until cold.
Makes 24-30

> NOTE
> • *If preferred, 250 ml (8 fl oz) oil may be used and the butter omitted – the texture will be less moist, rather like a biscuit.*

DATE, NUT AND OAT BISCUITS

125 g (4 oz) butter
100 g (3½ oz) caster sugar
1 egg, beaten
125 g (4 oz) stoned dates, chopped
60 g (2 oz) chopped walnuts or pecan nuts
125 g (4 oz) plain flour or brown bread flour
2.5 ml (½ tsp) baking powder
2.5 ml (½ tsp) bicarbonate of soda
pinch of salt
90 g (3 oz) rolled oats
45 g (1½ oz) desiccated coconut
few drops vanilla essence

Melt butter, add sugar and mix well. Pour into mixing bowl and add egg. Stir in dates together with walnuts or pecan nuts. Sift flour, baking powder, bicarbonate of soda and salt and add to butter mixture, tipping in any bran left in sieve. Add oats, coconut and vanilla. Mix well – the mixture will be soft, but firms up on cooling. Shape into small balls and place on lightly oiled baking trays, leaving room for spreading. Flatten lightly with a fork and bake at 180°C (350°F, gas 4) for 12 minutes or until golden brown. Cool on a wire rack.
Makes about 30

ALMOND MERINGUE FINGERS

2 egg whites
200 g (7 oz) caster sugar
60 g (2 oz) finely chopped almonds
plain chocolate (optional)

Whisk egg whites until fairly stiff. Whisk in sugar, a little at a time, and beat until mixture is stiff and glossy. Fold in almonds. Fill piping bag with mixture and, using a plain nozzle, pipe 7.5-cm (3-in) long fingers on to baking trays which have been oiled and dusted with cornflour. Bake at 140°C (275°F, gas 1) for 1½ hours, until pale beige in colour, then turn off oven and leave until cold before opening the door. If using the chocolate finish, melt plain chocolate with 5-10 ml (1-2 tsp) water and dip in the end of each meringue finger, turning to coat. Place on a wire rack to set.
Makes about 20

OAT AND COCONUT BISCUITS

Large, crunchy biscuits.

250 g (9 oz) soft butter
200 g (7 oz) demerara sugar
125 g (4 oz) brown bread flour
175 g (6 oz) rolled oats
90 g (3 oz) desiccated coconut
1.25 ml (¼ tsp) salt
few drops vanilla essence
2.5 ml (½ tsp) bicarbonate of soda
45 ml (3 tbsp) hot water

Cream butter and sugar very well. Add flour, oats, coconut, salt and vanilla. Dissolve bicarbonate of soda in the hot water and add. Mix well. Roll into small balls, or push from a teaspoon into rough heaps on oiled baking trays, leaving plenty of room for spreading. Flatten lightly with a fork and bake at l80°C (350°F, gas 4) for 15 minutes or until pale brown. Remove carefully, using a spatula, and leave on wire racks to crisp.
Makes about 36

QUICK FRUIT BARS

*Dark and fruity, nutty and chewy,
this recipe makes a big batch of
lunch-box specials.*

250 g (9 oz) self-raising flour
300 g (11 oz) demerara sugar
140 g (4½ oz) desiccated coconut
250 g (9 oz) mixed dried fruit
60 g (2 oz) chopped pecan nuts or
chopped, toasted almonds
2 eggs
few drops vanilla essence
125 g (4 oz) butter
100 ml (3½ fl oz) oil
15 ml (1 tbsp) cocoa powder
10 ml (2 tsp) ground mixed spice

In a large bowl mix flour, sugar, coconut, fruit and nuts. Stir in eggs beaten
with vanilla. Melt together the butter,
oil, cocoa and mixed spice over low
heat. Add to flour and fruit mixture and
mix well. Press firmly into an
oiled 25 x 20-cm (10 x 8-in) baking tin
(the batter will be rather moist and slippery, but this is correct) and bake at
180°C (350°F, gas 4) for 40 minutes until
firm. Cut into 24 jumbo bars or into
36 medium squares and cool in tin.
Makes 24-36

CHOCOLATE OAT
FRIDGE SQUARES

200 g (7 oz) caster sugar
75 ml (5 tbsp) cocoa powder
125 ml (4 fl oz) milk
125 g (4 oz) butter
125 g (4 oz) seedless raisins
pinch of salt
275 g (10 oz) rolled oats
90 g (3 oz) desiccated coconut
few drops vanilla essence

Put sugar, cocoa, milk, butter, raisins
and salt into heavy-based saucepan.
Bring to the boil over low heat, stirring
constantly. Simmer for about 5 minutes,
then remove from the hob and stir in the
oats, coconut and vanilla. Mix very well.
Spoon into a shallow, buttered dish,

Lemon Sesame Snaps (page 9); Almond Meringue Fingers; Fruit Drops.

patting mixture in to a thickness of
about 2.5 cm (1 in). Cool, then cut into
28 squares, using a knife dipped into
water. Store in the refrigerator.
Makes 28

NOTE
● *When melting chocolate, be
careful not to overheat it, and
do not stir. If too thick for easy
dipping, it may be thinned down
with just a dash of boiling water
and then stirred until smooth.*

GINGERBREAD MEN

Gingerbread 'people' are traditional party fare and may be simply decorated with currants for eyes and buttons down the middle of the body, or more elaborately iced after baking, using a very thin nozzle to pipe on hair, mouths, bow ties, collars, even shoes and aprons. If decorating before baking, it is important to brush the biscuit with unbeaten egg white, not only to secure the currants, but to provide a shiny finish. If you do not have a gingerbread cutter, use animal shapes or any other cutters.

125 g (4 oz) soft butter
100 g (3½ oz) demerara sugar
30 ml (2 tbsp) golden syrup
1 egg, lightly beaten
300 g (11 oz) plain flour
5 ml (1 tsp) bicarbonate of soda
15 ml (1 tbsp) ground ginger

SPECIAL DECORATIVE ICING
185-250 g (6½-9 oz) icing sugar
45 ml (3 tbsp) egg white (about
1 large egg)
6 drops lemon juice

Cream butter, sugar and syrup until light and fluffy. Beat in egg. Sift flour, bicarbonate of soda and ginger. Beat into creamed mixture, and when well mixed, knead lightly. Using a floured rolling pin, roll out on lightly floured board and cut into shapes. Arrange on oiled baking trays, apply egg white and currants and bake on middle shelf of oven at 180°C (350°F, gas 4) for about 10 minutes. Allow to cool on trays before removing to wire racks.

For the icing, sift icing sugar. Using a fork, beat egg white until foamy. Slowly beat in icing sugar, using a wooden spoon and beating well between additions. When a thick, piping consistency has been reached, beat in lemon juice. Pipe on to cooled gingerbread shapes as suggested, and leave on a wire rack to cool and set.

Gingerbread Men, Party Faces, gingerbread teddy bears and colourful meringue nests.

MERINGUES

Perfect meringues, pale and crisp, are not difficult to make and the following foolproof recipe may be used in a variety of different ways, with imaginative shapes and decorations making them ideal for children's parties. To ensure success, follow the instructions carefully.

4 egg whites at room temperature
12 drops lemon juice
200 g (7 oz) caster sugar
10 ml (2 tsp) cornflour

The mixing bowl (preferably not plastic) and beaters must be spotlessly clean and free from grease. Whisk egg whites with lemon juice to soft peak stage. While beating, add 150 g (5 oz) of the sugar, a little at a time, and beat until very stiff. Using a metal spoon, fold in remaining sugar and the cornflour. (The addition of cornflour helps to prevent weeping.) The mixture may now be spooned into a piping bag, or simply dropped in mounds, with a little peak to the tops, on to *ungreased* baking trays. (Simply line with ordinary greaseproof paper or waxed kitchen paper – the cooked meringues will peel off very easily.) Bake meringues on the middle shelf of the oven at 120°C (250°F, gas ½) for 1 hour – do not open the door at all. Turn oven off and leave inside until absolutely cold before removing and storing in an airtight tin.
Makes about 24 small shapes

VARIATIONS
Party Meringues
If using a piping bag, try one or more of the following ideas (none of which requires artificial food colouring) for children's parties.
- Using a plain nozzle, pipe out the letters of the alphabet.
- Pipe mixture into circles and sprinkle with chocolate vermicelli before baking, or pipe into logs, and dip one end of each baked log into melted chocolate when cold.
- Pipe into nests, and use as containers for small sweets.
- Using a fluted nozzle, pipe into 'caterpillars' with peaked tails. For the feelers, insert two small pieces of spaghetti and dust the body lightly with a little cocoa powder.
- For meringue mice, use a plain nozzle and pipe mixture into mounds, tapering front and back. Push two tiny segments of glacé cherry into the front, for the eyes, and two short lengths of spaghetti on either side for the whiskers. Use flaked almonds for the ears, and either spaghetti or a short strip of liquorice for the tail. (Some children are allergic to liquorice, therefore spaghetti is perhaps the better choice.)

Chocolate Meringues
Use 5 ml (1 tsp) cocoa powder for each egg white used, adding it to the sugar.

PARTY FACES

Cheerful cookies to brighten a birthday tea. Made from a basic dough, rolled and cut with a large round cutter, they may be decorated before baking, or left plain, then iced and decorated when cold. Use the suggestions below, or have fun fashioning your own funny faces. Artificially coloured icing is not necessary – the sweets and cherries are colourful enough and look best on plain white icing.

500 g (18 oz) plain flour
5 ml (1 tsp) baking powder
1.25 ml (¼ tsp) salt
200 g (7 oz) caster sugar
250 g (9 oz) butter
2 eggs
few drops vanilla essence

ICING
185 g (6½ oz) icing sugar, sifted
15 g (½ oz) soft butter
20 ml (4 tsp) boiling water

Sift flour, baking powder, salt and sugar. Rub in butter until finely crumbled. Beat eggs with vanilla and add. Mix well, then knead to a dough. Pat out on lightly floured board and then roll out fairly thinly, using a floured rolling pin. Cut into rounds with a 7.5-cm (3-in) cutter and place on oiled baking trays, leaving room for spreading. Re-roll and cut the trimmings. If desired, decorate biscuits before baking by brushing with unbeaten egg white and lightly pressing in segments of glacé cherries for the eyes, a currant or chocolate chip for the nose, and an almond strip for the mouth. Bake on middle shelf of oven at 180°C (350°F, gas 4) for 12 minutes, until pale gold and just beginning to colour round the edges. Remove to a wire rack to cool.

For the icing, combine all ingredients until smooth. Coat top of each baked biscuit smoothly, using a knife dipped into boiling water. Use Smarties or chocolate chips for eyes or noses, currants for eyes, liquorice or almond strips for eyebrows and mouths, and chocolate vermicelli for hair.
Makes about 40

GINGER-GLAZED SHORTBREAD

Delicious, gingery wedges, thinly covered with a fudgy glaze.

BASE
125 g (4 oz) soft butter
60 ml (4 tbsp) caster sugar
185 g (6½ oz) plain flour
5 ml (1 tsp) baking powder
10 ml (2 tsp) ground ginger

GLAZE
60 ml (4 tbsp) sifted icing sugar
30 g (1 oz) butter
2.5 ml (½ tsp) ground ginger
15 ml (1 tbsp) preserved ginger syrup

Cream butter and sugar until light. Sift dry ingredients and add. Mix well and then knead until mixture forms a ball. Pat out and press evenly into an un-greased, 23-cm (9-in) diameter, loose-bottomed cake tin. Prick well, press round the edge with the tines of a fork and mark into 12 wedges. Bake on middle shelf of the oven at 160°C (325°F, gas 3) for 40 minutes.

Just before end of baking time prepare glaze by combining ingredients in small saucepan. Heat very gently until just melted – on no account allow mixture to boil. Using the back of a spoon, spread hot mixture over hot, cooked base to within 2.5 cm (1 in) of the edge so that crimping remains visible. Cut through wedges and leave until cold. Cut again, push up base and remove. Decorate with slivers of preserved ginger if desired.
Makes 12 wedges

COCONUT SHORTBREAD FINGERS

An unusual shortbread with a slight twist to the flavour.

150 g (5 oz) plain flour
60 ml (4 tbsp) caster sugar
75 g (2½ oz) desiccated coconut
125 g (4 oz) soft butter, diced
extra caster sugar

Mix dry ingredients. Rub in butter thoroughly, using an electric beater, until mixture has a fine, crumbly consistency, then knead very well until dough clings together and forms a smooth ball. Press evenly into an ungreased, 23-cm (9-in) square baking tin, mark into 21 fingers and prick well. Bake on middle shelf of oven at 150°C (300°F, gas 2) for about 50-60 minutes. Cut through fingers, sprinkle with extra caster sugar and leave in tin until cold before removing.
Makes 21

RICH SCOTS SHORTBREAD

Traditional ingredients, and the traditional method, result in this picture-book, perfect shortbread, suitable for a special occasion. To shape, use decorative shortbread moulds if you have them. Dust the moulds with cornflour each time before pressing in the dough, and it will unmould easily. Alternatively, use a sandwich cake tin, as follows.

125 g (4 oz) soft butter
45 ml (3 tbsp) caster sugar
140 g (4½ oz) plain flour
25 ml (5 tsp) rice flour

Cream the butter, then slowly beat in the sugar. When well mixed, gradually add the flour sifted with rice flour. When thoroughly combined, knead gently until mixture holds together and forms a ball. Lightly dust an 18-cm (7-in) diameter sandwich cake tin with corn-

flour. Shake out the excess, then pat the shortbread dough in firmly and evenly. Turn out on to an ungreased baking tray by running a knife round the edges, turning the tin upside down, and giving it a hard shake. The shortbread 'cake' should drop out easily. If there is any cornflour on the top, use a pastry brush to remove. Crimp edges with forefinger and thumb, prick well and score lightly into eight wedges. Bake on middle shelf of oven at 150°C (300°F, gas 2) for 45 minutes until palest beige in colour. Dust with a little extra caster sugar, cut through the wedges and leave until cold before removing.
Makes 8 wedges

SHORTBREAD PENNIES

If you don't have a wooden stamp, preferably with a thistle design, or a shortbread mould, simply prick each round twice with the tines of a fork to resemble buttons, in which case they are called Shortbread Buttons.

150 g (5 oz) plain flour
25 ml (5 tsp) cornflour
45 g (1½ oz) icing sugar
125 g (4 oz) soft butter
few drops vanilla essence
caster sugar

Sift flour, cornflour and icing sugar. Rub in butter until mixture is very finely crumbled. Add vanilla and knead well to a smooth dough. This takes several minutes. Pat out on unfloured board and then roll lightly with a rolling pin to flatten evenly, 5-mm (¼-in) thick. Cut into rounds, using a 4 or 5-cm (1½ or 2-in) cutter. It is important that the rounds be of uniform thickness. Gather up trimmings, knead, pat out and cut until all the dough has been used. Place rounds on ungreased baking tray and either stamp or prick as suggested. Bake at 150°C (300°F, gas 2) for about 30 minutes until deep gold in colour. Do not allow to brown. Remove to a wire rack and sift caster sugar over the short-bread while warm.
Makes 22-24

Ginger-glazed Shortbread; Shortbread Pennies; Melt-away Shortbread.

SPICY SHORTBREAD

This shortbread is made with oil.

200 g (7 oz) plain flour
45 g (1½ oz) cornflour
pinch of salt
5 ml (1 tsp) grated nutmeg (scant)
100 g (3½ oz) caster sugar
150 ml (¼ pt) oil
TOPPING
5 ml (1 tsp) caster sugar mixed with
pinch of ground cinnamon

Sift dry ingredients. Add oil and knead until smooth. Press dough on to ungreased base of 23-cm (9-in) diameter, loose-bottomed cake tin. Use a rolling pin to flatten evenly. Mark into 12 wedges, prick well, crimp edges and sprinkle with topping. Leave to stand for about 30 minutes. Bake at 150°C (300°F, gas 2) for 45 minutes. Cut right through wedges, but leave on base of tin until cold and crisp.
Makes 12 wedges

MOCHA PECAN SHORTBREAD

125 g (4 oz) soft butter
60 ml (4 tbsp) caster sugar
10 ml (2 tsp) instant coffee granules
10 ml (2 tsp) water
150 g (5 oz) plain flour
45 ml (3 tbsp) cornflour
45-75 ml (3-5 tbsp) finely chopped
pecan nuts

Using an electric beater, cream butter. Slowly add sugar, beating until light and fluffy. Beat in coffee dissolved in water. Sift flour with cornflour and add slowly, beating all the time. When the mixture becomes moist and forms a ball, add nuts and knead well. Press into an ungreased 18-cm (7-in) square baking tin, prick well and mark into 18 fingers. Bake on middle shelf of oven at 150°C (300°F, gas 2) for 45 minutes. Cut through and leave in tin until cold.
Makes 18

MELT-AWAY SHORTBREAD

A basic, flop-proof recipe.

250 g (9 oz) soft butter
100 g (3½ oz) caster sugar
300 g (11 oz) plain flour
75 g (2½ oz) cornflour
extra caster sugar

Cream butter. Slowly add sugar, beating well until pale and fluffy. Sift flour with cornflour and slowly beat into butter mixture to make a soft and creamy dough. Press evenly into an ungreased, 33 x 20-cm (13 x 8-in) Swiss roll tin. Prick well, mark lightly into fingers and then bake at 150°C (300°F, gas 2) for 45 minutes until a pale biscuit colour. Remove from oven and cut through fingers. Sprinkle lightly with caster sugar and leave in tin until cold. Remove and store in airtight container.
Makes about 30

YEAST BREADS

WHITE FARMHOUSE BREAD

Instant yeast reduces the rising time of bread, and I have used it here to make a high, attractive flour-topped loaf. The 'farmhouse' effect comes from slashing the unbaked loaf lengthwise – as it rises in the oven the slashes open out. Baked in a smaller tin than usual, the result is a loaf with a high, humped fan-like top. However, the dough may be used in more conventional ways if preferred.

10 ml (2 tsp) instant dry yeast
500 g (18 oz) white bread flour
5 ml (1 tsp) salt
7.5 ml (1½ tsp) caster sugar
30 g (1 oz) butter
325 ml (11 fl oz) warm water

In a large bowl mix yeast, flour sifted with salt, and sugar. Rub in butter. Add water. Mix, first with a wooden spoon and then with the hands, to make a kneadable dough, adding about 20 ml (4 tsp) extra warm water if necessary. Knead in the bowl for about 5 minutes, until soft and pliable, then cover bowl with a damp cloth and leave to rest for 30 minutes in a warm place. Oil a 20 x 10 x 6-cm (8 x 4 x 2½-in) loaf tin.

Punch dough down and form into a loaf by pressing dough out to the length of the tin, and three times the width. Fold over, sides to middle, and drop into tin, seam side down. Press dough evenly out into the corners. Cover loosely with oiled plastic wrap and leave to rise for 30 minutes until dough reaches just over the top of the tin. Using a sharp knife, make several deep slits lengthwise along the top of the loaf and sift over a little flour. Bake on middle shelf of oven at 200°C (400°F, gas 6) for 30 minutes until well-risen and the slashes have burst open. Turn out on to a wire rack to cool.
Makes 1 loaf

*Italian Herb Bread (page 39);
Cheese-topped Onion Crown Loaf (page 40); White Farmhouse Bread;
Baker's Pride Bread (page 39).*

BASIC WHITE BREAD

Baking one's own bread is one of the ultimate culinary pleasures – from the fermenting of the yeast and the rising of the dough, to the final, aromatic waft of a crusty loaf. However, yeast breads cannot be hurried. A good rising, especially the second one, is vital.

875 g (1¾ lb) white bread flour
10 ml (2 tsp) salt
30 g (1 oz) butter
10 ml (2 tsp) caster sugar
625 ml (21 fl oz) warm water
15 ml (1 tbsp) dried yeast

GLAZE
1 egg white lightly mixed with
5 ml (1 tsp) water

Sift flour and salt into a large bowl. Rub in butter. Dissolve the sugar in 250 ml (8 fl oz) of the water. Sprinkle the yeast on the top, cover and leave for about 10 minutes until frothy. Make a well in centre of flour mixture, pour in yeast mixture, mix, and then add remaining water. Mix to a dough – you may need just a little extra water. Turn on to a lightly floured board and knead very well, for about 10 minutes, until smooth and elastic. Brush a large bowl with oil, turn the ball of dough in it to coat, then cover and leave to rise in a warm place for about 1½ hours until doubled. (To test, press deeply with one finger – the dent should remain.)

Punch down and knead briefly, then break off two-thirds of the dough. Knead into a loaf and place in an oiled, 20 x 13 x 7.5- cm (8 x 5 x 3-in) loaf tin. Brush top with glaze, cover lightly and leave for about 1½ hours or until dough reaches to 2 cm (¾ in) above top of tin. Brush again with glaze and bake at 220°C (425°F, gas 7) for 15 minutes. Reduce heat to 200°C (400°F, gas 6) and bake another 35 minutes. Turn out on to a wire rack – if you rap the bottom of the loaf, it should sound hollow. Leave on a wire rack to cool. To make a Vienna Double Plait, roll remaining dough into six long sausages of equal length. Make two plaits, place one on top of the other,

dampen ends and pinch to seal. Cover lightly and leave to rise for about 1½ hours until doubled. Place on oiled baking tray, brush with milk, sprinkle with poppy seeds and bake at 220°C (425°F, gas 7) for 10 minutes, then at 180°C (350°F, gas 4) for 20 minutes. Break into chunks to serve
Makes 2 loaves

WHITE HERB BREAD PLAIT

For extra lightness use half white bread flour and half plain flour.

875 g (1¾ lb) sifted white bread flour
10 ml (2 tsp) salt
30 g (1 oz) melted butter
100 ml (7 tbsp) chopped parsley
1 small onion, finely chopped
5 ml (1 tsp) dried thyme
2 cloves garlic, crushed
10 ml (2 tsp) caster sugar
about 600 ml (1 pint) warm water
15 ml (1 tbsp) dried yeast
grated Parmesan cheese and
poppy seeds

Sift flour with salt. Add butter, onion, garlic and herbs. Stir sugar into 250 ml (8 fl oz) of the water, sprinkle in the yeast, cover and leave to froth. Pour the yeast mixture into a well in the flour, mix and add the remaining water or enough to make a workable dough. Knead until smooth and elastic. Shape into a ball and return to bowl. Brush top with oil, cover and leave to rise in a warm place until doubled, about 45 minutes.

Punch down, knead well and then divide into two. Divide each half into three, roll into long sausages and then plait, pinching to close at both ends. Place loaves on oiled baking trays, cover lightly with damp cloth and leave to rise until doubled – 30 to 60 minutes. Brush with milk and sprinkle with Parmesan and poppy seeds. Bake at 220°C (425°F, gas 7) for 10 minutes, then reduce heat to 180°C (350°F, gas 4) and bake for a further 20 minutes.
Makes 2 large plaits

POPPY SEED PLAIT

This recipe makes a beautifully big, rich white plait, but it requires three risings, so allow plenty of time.

250 ml (8 fl oz) warm water
30 ml (2 tbsp) caster sugar
10 ml (2 tsp) dried yeast
500 g (18 oz) white bread flour
5ml (1 tsp) salt
25 ml (5 tsp) oil
2 eggs, beaten
poppy seeds

Pour 60 ml (4 tbsp) of the water into a mug. Stir in 5 ml (1 tsp) of the sugar and then sprinkle in the yeast. Cover and leave to froth. Sift flour and salt. Add remaining sugar. Quickly stir yeast mixture and pour into well in centre of flour mixture. Stir to mix, then add oil, eggs and remaining water. Mix to a workable dough – you may need a dash more water. Turn on to floured board and knead for 10 minutes until very smooth and pale khaki in colour. Shape into a ball, brush a bowl with oil and turn dough in it until coated. Cover and leave to rise until doubled, about 1¼ hours.

Punch down, cover and leave to rise again until doubled. Divide dough into three, roll into 40-cm (16-in) long sausages, and plait. Pinch ends firmly together and place on oiled baking tray. Cover loosely with oiled plastic wrap and leave to rise until doubled, about 45 minutes. Brush top with milk and sprinkle with poppy seeds. Bake just above centre of oven at 200°C (400°F, gas 6) for 10 minutes, then at 180°C (350°F, gas 4) for 20 minutes. Carefully transfer to a wire rack to cool.
Makes 1 loaf

FRENCH BREAD

Home-bakers cannot produce those typical French baguettes. The technique differs from that of ordinary bread, and the equipment can be quite daunting. This fairly quick and easy recipe will produce two fine loaves or bâtards. *French bread contains no sugar, butter or oil, so eat it on the day of baking.*

15 ml (1 tbsp) dried yeast
400 ml (14 fl oz) warm water
310 g (11½ oz) plain flour
310 g (11½ oz) white bread flour
5ml (1 tsp) salt
sesame seeds

Sprinkle yeast into 125 ml (4 fl oz) of the water, cover and leave to stand for about 15 minutes until frothy. Sift flours and salt into a large bowl. Stir the bubbly yeast and pour into well in centre of sifted mixture. Mix and then slowly add the remaining water, making a fairly soft dough. Another 5-10 ml (1-2 tsp) water may be necessary. Knead vigorously for 10 minutes on lightly floured board. Return to bowl, cover loosely with a damp cloth and leave to rise in a warm place for about 2 hours or until just more than doubled. Prod with two fingers – the indentations should remain. Knock down and knead hard for a few minutes.

Divide into two balls, cover and stand for 10 minutes. Roll balls into two 37-cm (15-in) long sausages and place on floured cloth. Tuck cloth tightly up against sides to prevent loaves from spreading sideways. Cover loosely with a cloth and leave to rise for 1-1½ hours until nearly doubled in height.

Without touching the loaves, roll them very gently on to a non-stick baking tray so that they lie upside down. Remove any traces of flour with pastry brush. Slash tops three times diagonally, brush with water and sprinkle with sesame seeds. For a shiny, crisp crust, place pan of boiling water at bottom of a 220°C (425°F, gas 7) oven. Bake loaves just above centre of oven for 15 minutes. Reduce heat to 180°C (350°F, gas 4) and bake for 20 minutes. Cool on a wire rack.
Makes 2 loaves

WHITE RING BREAD

Similar to the Greek Kouloura *Ring, this is a plain but attractive loaf, baked in a ring tin and rising into a high ring with a nice brown crust, strewn with poppy seeds.*

20 ml (4 tsp) caster sugar
60 ml (4 tbsp) warm water
10 ml (2 tsp) dried yeast
250 ml (8 fl oz) milk
15 g (½ oz) butter
1 egg, beaten
375 g (13 oz) white bread flour
5 ml (1 tsp) salt
poppy seeds

Dissolve 5 ml (1 tsp) of the sugar in the water, sprinkle in the yeast, cover and leave to froth. Meanwhile scald the milk, add butter and remaining sugar and cool to lukewarm. Stir in egg, reserving 5 ml (1 tsp). Sift flour with salt into mixing bowl. Stir frothy yeast and pour into well in centre of flour. Mix, then add milk mixture and combine well to a very soft dough. Turn on to well-floured board and knead for 10 minutes, adding about 60 ml (4 tbsp) extra flour in stages, as it becomes necessary. When dough is smooth and pliable and no longer sticky, shape into a ball and place in oiled bowl, turning to coat. Cover and leave to rise until doubled, about 1¼ hours.

Punch down and knead for 1 minute, then roll into a long, smooth sausage. Coil the sausage in oiled, 20-cm (8-in) diameter x 7.5-cm (3-in) deep spring ring tin, joining ends firmly by first brushing with a little of the reserved beaten egg. Press dough down evenly – the tin should be half full. Cover and leave until dough has risen to just over the top – about 1¼ hours. Brush top with the remaining egg and sprinkle liberally with poppy seeds. Place a pan of hot water on bottom shelf of oven, and bake bread in centre of oven at 200°C (400°F, gas 6) for 10 minutes. Cover loosely with a sheet of greaseproof paper and bake for a further 30 minutes at 180°C (350°F, gas 4). Release spring of tin and turn out to cool on a wire rack.
Makes 1 loaf

ITALIAN HERB BREAD

A fragrant round loaf, baked in a cake tin. This is not a standard bread dough, and it takes longer to rise than usual, but the reward is in the eating. Break into crusty chunks, and serve warm with butter and a bowl of hot soup.

5ml (1 tsp) caster sugar
60 ml (4 tbsp) warm water
10 ml (2 tsp) dried yeast
125 ml (4 fl oz) milk
30 g (1oz) butter
1 egg, beaten
375 g (13 oz) white bread flour
5ml (1 tsp) salt
75 ml (5 tbsp) finely chopped parsley
2-3 large cloves garlic, crushed
4 spring onions, plus some of
the tops, chopped
5 ml (1 tsp) dried oregano
25 ml (5 tsp) grated Parmesan cheese

Stir sugar into water, sprinkle in yeast, cover and leave to froth. Scald milk, remove from hob, add butter and when melted, stir in egg. Cool to lukewarm. Sift 250 g (9 oz) of the flour with the salt into a bowl. Stir the bubbly yeast and pour into a well in centre of flour mixture. Mix and add the milk mixture. Stir in parsley, garlic, spring onions and oregano. When well combined, sift in remaining flour. Mix with hands until dough holds together and then turn on to floured board and knead for about 5-10 minutes until dough forms a pliable ball. Brush the bowl with oil and turn the dough in it to coat, then cover and leave until well risen, about 2 hours.

Punch down and knead lightly. Place in a 20-cm (8-in) diameter, 6-cm (2½-in) deep oiled cake tin, pressing in vigorously with fingers to spread out to sides in a flat, level cake. The tin should be one-third full. Cover with a cloth and leave to rise for 1½ hours or until dough fills two-thirds of tin. Brush with milk and sprinkle with Parmesan, then bake on middle shelf at 200°C (400°F, gas 6) for 10 minutes, then at 180°C (350°F, gas 4) for 25 minutes. Turn out on to a wire rack to cool.
Makes 1 loaf

Italian Herb Bread and Baker's Pride Bread are both delicious with soup.

BAKER'S PRIDE BREAD

A big, savoury loaf, so easy to make, but really impressive.

500 g (18 oz) white bread flour
10 ml (2 tsp) instant dry yeast
5ml (1 tsp) salt
7.5 ml (1½ tsp) mixed dried herbs
1 small onion, finely chopped
100 ml (7 tbsp) chopped parsley
10 ml (2 tsp) caster sugar
15 ml (1 tbsp) oil
450 ml (¾ pint) warm water
caraway seeds

Mix the flour, yeast, salt, herbs, onion, parsley and sugar in large bowl. Stir oil into water and add to flour mixture. Mix to a tacky batter, then turn into an oiled, 20 x 13 x 7.5-cm (8 x 5 x 3-in) loaf tin. The batter will be quite headstrong and elastic – use a dampened rubber spatula to press it in evenly. Sprinkle top with caraway seeds. Leave to rise, uncovered, until dough rises to just above the top of tin – 35-45 minutes. Bake at 200°C (400°F, gas 6) for 30 minutes, then at 180°C (350°F, gas 4) for 30 minutes. Turn out and cool on a wire rack.
Makes 1 large loaf

Cheese-topped Onion Crown Loaf

The risen dough is shaped into balls and arranged in a cake tin for proving, where they join into a circle of buns with humped tops.

5ml (1 tsp) caster sugar
200 ml (7 fl oz) warm water
7.5 ml (1½ tsp) dried yeast
250 g (9 oz) white bread flour
5ml (1 tsp) salt
125 g (4 oz) wholewheat flour
1 large onion, finely chopped and sautéed in a little oil
100 ml (7 tbsp) finely chopped parsley
15 g (½ oz) butter

TOPPING
75 ml (5 tbsp) finely grated Cheddar cheese
plenty of milled black pepper

Stir sugar into water, sprinkle in yeast, cover and leave to froth. Sift white flour with salt. Add wholewheat flour, onion and parsley. Rub in butter. Stir frothy yeast and pour into well in centre of dry ingredients. Mix to a dough, first with a wooden spoon and then with the hands. Turn on to floured board and knead for 5 minutes to a soft and elastic ball. Place in oiled bowl, turn to coat, then cover and leave to rise until doubled, about 1 hour.

Punch down, cover and rest for 10 minutes. Divide into six and roll each into a smooth ball. Place five of the balls in a ring around the sides of an oiled, 20-cm (8-in) diameter x 6-cm (2½-in) deep cake tin, spacing them equally. Place the sixth ball in the centre. Cover loosely with oiled plastic wrap and leave to prove for about 45 minutes, until rolls reach top of tin and are all joined together. Brush with milk, sprinkle with cheese and grind the pepper over. Bake just above centre of oven at 200°C (400°F, gas 6) for 10 minutes, then at 180°C (350°F, gas 4) for 35 minutes. Run a knife round the circumference and turn on to a wire rack to cool. Serve by breaking buns apart.
Makes 1 loaf

Cheese and Caraway Cottage Loaf

This quaintly shaped loaf is lightly flavoured with caraway and enriched with cheese and skimmed milk powder. These two ingredients may be omitted for a lighter-textured loaf.

10 ml (2 tsp) caster sugar
350 ml (12 fl oz) warm water
10 ml (2 tsp) dried yeast
500 g (18 oz) white bread flour
10 ml (2 tsp) salt
10 ml (2 tsp) dry mustard
45 g (1½ oz) skimmed milk powder
5 ml (1 tsp) caraway seeds
300 ml finely grated Cheddar cheese

Mix sugar into water, sprinkle in yeast, cover and leave to froth. Sift flour, salt, mustard and milk powder. Add caraway seeds and 250 ml of the cheese. Stir yeast and pour into well in centre of dry ingredients. Mix well, adding about 10 ml (2 tsp) warm water to make a kneadable dough. Turn on to lightly floured board and knead 5-8 minutes until smooth and elastic. Place in bowl brushed with oil, turn to coat, cover and leave to rise for 1¼ - 1½ hours until doubled. (Due to the extra ingredients this dough has a slow rising period.)

Punch down, cover and rest for 10 minutes. Pinch off three-quarters of the dough and shape it into a flat 18-cm (7-in) diameter circle, using a rolling pin to get it really level. Brush with milk. Form the remaining piece of dough into a ball and place on top of the base. Push the handle of a wooden spoon right through the centre, from the top to the bottom, to keep the ball in place. Remove the spoon and place the loaf in oiled, 23-cm (9-in) square tin – this prevents the base from spreading too much – then cover loosely with oiled plastic wrap and leave to prove for about 45 minutes until doubled. Brush with milk, sprinkle with remaining cheese, and bake on middle shelf of oven at 200°C (400°F, gas 6) for 30 minutes. Cover loosely with greaseproof paper if over-browning. Cool on a wire rack.
Makes 1 loaf

Spiced Fruit Plait

75 g (2½ oz) seedless raisins
60 g (2 oz) currants
45 ml (3 tbsp) mixed peel
25 ml (5 tsp) dark rum
25 ml (5 tsp) caster sugar
125 ml (4 fl oz) warm water
10 ml (2 tsp) dried yeast
310 g (11½ oz) white bread flour
2.5 ml (½ tsp) salt
2.5 ml (½ tsp) ground mixed spice
5 ml (1 tsp) ground cinnamon
30 g (1 oz) butter
1 egg, beaten

GLAZE
5ml (1 tsp) caster sugar
10 ml (2 tsp) boiling water

Place fruit and rum in a bowl, stir, cover and stand for 1 hour. In another bowl stir sugar into water, sprinkle in the yeast, cover and leave to froth.

Sift flour, salt and spices together. Rub in butter. Add egg to frothy yeast, mix well, then pour into well in centre of dry ingredients. Stir until flour is thoroughly moistened, then knead hard for about 5-10 minutes. Cover and rest dough for 10 minutes, then add soaked fruit. At first this seems like too much fruit, but keep kneading and eventually it will all be taken up by the dough, leaving the sides of the bowl quite clean. Cover and leave to rise in a warm place until doubled, about 1½ hours.

Punch down and divide into three. Roll each portion out into a 40-cm (16-in) long sausage. Make a plait, tucking the ends under, and place on oiled baking tray. Cover lightly and leave to rise in a warm place for about 1 hour or until doubled (test by prodding with one finger – the dent should remain).

Bake at 220°C (425°F, gas 7) for 10 minutes, then reduce heat to 180°C (350°F, gas 4) and bake for 20 minutes, covering the top loosely with a sheet of foil, shiny side out, when sufficiently browned. Cool on a wire rack and glaze while warm, not hot. To make the glaze, dissolve sugar in the water and brush over the top of the loaf.
Makes 1 loaf

SWEDISH TEA RING

125 ml (4 fl oz) milk
45 g (1½ oz) butter
7.5 ml (1½ tsp) dried yeast
45 ml (3 tbsp) warm water
45 ml (3 tbsp) caster sugar
1 egg, beaten
300 g (11 oz) plain flour
2.5 ml (½ tsp) salt

FILLING
20 ml (4 tsp) melted butter
30 ml (2 tbsp) caster sugar
75 g (2½ oz) mixed dried fruit
6 glacé cherries, chopped
2.5 ml (½ tsp) ground cinnamon
2.5 ml (½ tsp) ground mixed spice

Scald milk, add butter and cool to luke-warm. Sprinkle yeast into warm water, cover and leave to froth. Stir sugar and egg into milk mixture. Sift flour and salt, stir frothy yeast and pour into a well in centre of flour. Add milk mixture and mix to a soft dough. Knead on a floured board for 5-8 minutes, slowly adding extra flour as necessary until dough becomes smooth and pliable. Return to bowl, brush top with oil, cover with a damp cloth and leave to rise in a warm place for 1 hour 20 minutes or until doubled.

Punch down, knead for 1 minute, then cover and rise again for 30 minutes. Roll out on floured board to a large rectangle, about 5-mm (¼-in) thick. Brush entire surface with melted butter. Sprinkle with sugar, fruit and spices, then roll up tightly, like a Swiss roll. Curve into a ring, about 23 cm (9 in) in diameter, joining ends firmly with dampened fingers. Lift carefully on to an oiled baking tray. Using kitchen scissors, snip top at 3-cm (1¼-in) intervals, cutting half way through dough. Cover loosely with oiled plastic wrap and leave until well risen, about 45 minutes.

Bake on middle shelf of oven at 200°C (400°F, gas 6) for 10 minutes, then at 180°C (350°F, gas 4) for 15 minutes. Place greaseproof paper over the top when lightly browned. Cool for a few minutes on the tray, then transfer to a wire rack. Ice and decorate when cold.
Makes 1 ring loaf

This colourful Swedish Tea Ring and Spiced Fruit Plait will draw many compliments.

HEALTH BREADS

NUTTY BROWN BLOOMER LOAF

A beautiful bread, incorporating two flours, wheat germ and sunflower seeds. It requires only one rising, which is quite lengthy due to the unrefined ingredients, but it is nevertheless easy to make and is tops on the taste test.

375 g (13 oz) wholewheat flour
10 ml (2 tsp) salt
15 ml (1 tbsp) instant dry yeast
350 ml (12 fl oz) warm water
25 ml (5 tsp) honey
25 ml (5 tsp) oil
250 g (9 oz) white bread flour
45 g (1½ oz) wheat germ
60 g (2 oz) sunflower seeds

In a large bowl combine 185 g (6½ oz) of the wholewheat flour, salt and instant yeast. Mix water, honey and oil. Stir into flour mixture and mix to a sloppy dough. Cover and rest for 10 minutes. Add remaining wholewheat flour, the white flour, wheat germ and sunflower seeds. Mix with a wooden spoon and then with the hands to form a dough, adding up to 75 ml (5 tbsp) extra warm water as necessary. Knead in the bowl for 8-10 minutes – this is a firm dough which requires some hard kneading. When mixture forms a smooth ball and leaves the sides of the bowl clean, shape into a 25 x 13-cm (10 x 5-in) bloomer (or slab) with blunt ends.

Place on oiled baking tray, and tuck two cloths tightly on either side so that the dough rises upwards rather than sideways. Make six deep diagonal slashes across the top, cover loosely with oiled plastic wrap and leave to rise for 1 hour or until doubled. Brush with milk and bake on middle shelf of oven at 200°C (400°F, gas 6) for 30 minutes. Cool on a wire rack, and brush top with melted butter for a shiny finish.
Makes 1 loaf

FROM THE BACK: *Nutty Brown Bloomer Loaf; Caraway Rye Loaf; Brown Herb Bread Plait; Buttermilk Wholewheat Soda Bread with Rosemary.*

BROWN HERB BREAD PLAIT

This is a rewarding bread to bake, rising beautifully to a fat and chunky plait, topped with crushed wheat and lightly flavoured with herbs. The addition of a little soya flour is optional, but it adds nutrition and helps to keep the loaf fresh. Break into chunks to serve.

300 ml (½ pint) warm water
10 ml (2 tsp) dried yeast
250 g (9 oz) white bread flour
250 g (9 oz) wholewheat flour
45 ml (3 tbsp) soya flour (optional)
10 ml (2 tsp) dried mixed herbs
5 ml (1 tsp) salt
25 ml (5 tsp) oil
25 ml (5 tsp) honey

TOPPING
30 ml (2 tbsp) crushed wheat
1.25 ml (¼ tsp) mixed dried herbs

Pour 125 ml (4 fl oz) of the water into a mug. Sprinkle in yeast, cover and leave to froth. Mix white bread, wholewheat and soya flours in large bowl. Add herbs, salt, oil and honey. Stir the risen yeast and pour into a well in centre of dry ingredients. Add remaining water, or just enough to make a workable dough. Turn on to floured board and knead well for 10 minutes, re-flouring the board when necessary – the dough is inclined to be sticky. When the dough forms a smooth ball, place it in a bowl brushed with oil, turn to coat, cover and leave in a warm place to rise until doubled, about 1-1½ hours.

Punch down, cover and rest for about 10 minutes. Divide into three and roll into 35-cm (14-in) long sausages. Make a plait, pinching ends to join firmly. Cover loosely with oiled plastic wrap and leave to prove until doubled, about 45 minutes. Brush top with milk and sprinkle with crushed wheat and herbs. Bake just above centre of oven at 200°C (400°F, gas 6) for 10 minutes, then at 180°C (350°F, gas 4) for 20 minutes. Cool on a wire rack.
Makes 1 loaf

WHOLEWHEAT BATONS WITH GARLIC AND FRESH HERBS

These French-style batons are excellent with soups, cheese or pâté.

10 ml (2 tsp) honey
300 ml (½ pint) warm water
10 ml (2 tsp) dried yeast
250 g (9 oz) white bread flour
5 ml (1 tsp) salt
250 g (9 oz) wholewheat flour
4 cloves garlic, crushed
45 ml (3 tbsp) finely chopped parsley
5 ml (1 tsp) chopped fresh rosemary needles
10 fresh sage leaves, chopped
5 ml (1 tsp) finely chopped fresh oregano leaves
beaten egg, sesame and poppy seeds

Dissolve honey in water. Sprinkle in the yeast, cover and leave to froth. Sift white flour with salt into a large bowl. Add wholewheat flour, garlic and all the herbs and mix well. Pour frothy yeast into a well in the centre and work in the flour until incorporated. Turn on to lightly floured board and knead hard for 10 minutes. Shape into a ball, return to bowl, brush top with oil, cover and leave to rise in a warm place for about 1½ hours or until doubled.

Punch down and divide into two. Shape each piece into a 28-cm (11-in) long baton and place on an oiled baking tray. With a sharp knife slash the tops three times, diagonally, and leave to rise until nearly doubled, about 1¼ hours. Brush with beaten egg and sprinkle with sesame and poppy seeds in alternate, diagonal stripes. Bake just above centre of oven at 220°C (425°F, gas 7) for 10 minutes, then at 180°C (350°F, gas 4) for 15 minutes. Cool on a wire rack.
Makes 2 loaves

> HINT
> ● *Remember to remove the oiled plastic wrap on top of a risen loaf before baking.*

WHOLEWHEAT NUT, RAISIN AND YOGHURT BREAD

A superb, nutritious snack-time loaf.

125 g (4 oz) white bread flour
5 ml (1 tsp) salt
7.5 ml (1½ tsp) bicarbonate of soda
5 ml (1 tsp) ground cinnamon
2.5 ml (½ tsp) grated nutmeg
1.25 ml (¼ tsp) ground cloves
375 g (13 oz) wholewheat flour
25 ml (5 tsp) oil
25 ml (5 tsp) honey
45 ml (3 tbsp) demerara sugar
75 g (2½ oz) seedless raisins
40-60 g (1½-2 oz) finely chopped
walnuts, pecan or Brazil nuts
500 ml (17 fl oz) natural
drinking yoghurt

TOPPING
2.5 ml (½ tsp) ground cinnamon
25 ml (5 tsp) demerara sugar

Sift white flour with salt, bicarbonate of soda and spices. Mix in wholewheat flour, oil, honey, sugar, raisins and nuts. Stir in yoghurt, using a wooden spoon. Rinse the carton with 25 ml (5 tsp) water and add. Mix all the ingredients very well, then turn the batter into an oiled, 23 x 13 x 7.5-cm (9 x 5 x 3-in) loaf tin, spreading evenly. Sprinkle cinnamon and sugar over the top, and bake on middle shelf of oven at 180°C (350°F, gas 4) for 1 hour. Stand for 5 minutes before turning out on to a wire rack to cool.
Makes 1 loaf

HINT
● *Baking bread with a pan of water placed low down in the oven will produce a crisp crust.*
● *Be wary of adding too much water to a batter bread. If you make it too wet, the loaf will deflate in the oven. The consistency should be fairly thick and moist, almost like a fruit cake mixture.*

WHOLEWHEAT HONEY BREAD

15 ml (3 tsp) instant dry yeast
30 g (1 oz) wheat germ
500 g (18 oz) wholewheat flour
75 g (2½ oz) seedless raisins
5 ml (1 tsp) salt
45 g (1½ oz) sunflower seeds
about 500 ml (17 fl oz) warm water
45 ml (3 tbsp) honey
15 ml (1 tbsp) oil

Mix yeast, wheat germ, flour, raisins, salt and sunflower seeds in a large mixing bowl. Whisk 250 ml (8 fl oz) of the water with honey and oil. Pour into the dry ingredients and mix, then add remaining water, or enough to make a batter with the consistency of a fruit cake. Turn the batter into an oiled, 20 x 13 x 7.5-cm (8 x 5 x 3-in) loaf tin, and cover loosely with oiled plastic wrap. Leave in a warm place until batter rises to just over the top of the tin – about 30 minutes. Bake at 200°C (400°F, gas 6) for 30 minutes, then reduce heat to 180°C (350°F, gas 4) and bake for 20 minutes. Turn out on to a wire rack to cool.
Makes 1 large loaf

BUTTERMILK WHOLEWHEAT SODA BREAD WITH ROSEMARY

Soda bread is a traditional Scottish bread, served on Burns Night with Finnan Haddie Soup and Haggis. I have flavoured it with fresh rosemary. Serve freshly baked, broken into quarters, with butter.

250 g (9 oz) plain flour
5 ml (1 tsp) salt
5 ml (1 tsp) bicarbonate of soda
5 ml (1 tsp) caster sugar
250 g (9 oz) wholewheat flour
15 ml (1 tbsp) finely chopped fresh
rosemary needles
30 g (1 oz) butter
about 400 ml (14 fl oz) buttermilk

Sift plain flour with salt and bicarbonate of soda. Add sugar, wholewheat flour and rosemary. Rub in butter. Add buttermilk and mix to a soft dough. Shape into two 15-cm (6-in) diameter rounds, and place on a floured baking tray. Using the back of a knife, score deeply into quarters. Brush tops with beaten egg (milk may be used, but egg gives a better colour) and bake at 200°C (400°F, gas 6) for 30 minutes.
Makes 2 loaves

ENRICHED BATTER BREAD

A delicious, healthy loaf.

25 ml (5 tsp) honey
475 ml (16 fl oz) warm water
10 ml (2 tsp) dried yeast
375 g (13 oz) wholewheat flour
75 g (2½ oz) crushed wheat
75 ml (5 tbsp) soya flour
75 ml (5 tbsp) fat-free milk powder
30 g (1 oz) wheat germ
125 g (4 oz) brown bread flour
7.5 ml (1½ tsp) salt
25 ml (5 tsp) oil
sunflower seeds

Dissolve honey in 125 ml (4 fl oz) of the water. Sprinkle in the yeast, cover and leave to froth. Mix the remaining ingredients (except sunflower seeds). Give the yeast a quick stir and pour into a well in the centre of the dry ingredients. Mix, using a wooden spoon, and gradually add the remaining water, or just enough to give you a thick, sticky batter. Turn the batter into an oiled, 23 x 13 x 7.5-cm (9 x 5 x 3-in) loaf tin, making it nearly two-thirds full. Sprinkle the top thickly with sunflower seeds, pressing them in lightly. Cover loosely with oiled plastic wrap and leave to rise in a warm place for 45-60 minutes. Bake on middle shelf of oven at 200°C (400°F, gas 6) for 15 minutes, then at 180°C (350°F, gas 4) for 45-60 minutes. Stand for a few minutes before running a knife round edges. Cool on a wire rack.
Makes 1 loaf

PUMPERNICKEL BREAD

This is an unusual dark bread made with a variety of flours and interesting ingredients which could include mashed potato, caraway seeds, chocolate and coffee powder. The following is a delectable, fairly sweet version, containing a sprinkling of fruit, honey and molasses, with the cocoa and coffee providing colour rather than flavour.

300 ml (½ pint) warm water
25 ml (5 tsp) molasses
45 ml (3 tbsp) thin honey
10 ml (2 tsp) dried yeast
10 ml (2 tsp) instant coffee granules
10 ml (2 tsp) salt
15 ml (1 tbsp) cocoa powder
25 ml (5 tsp) melted butter
225 g (8 oz) rye flour
185 g (6½ oz) white bread flour
125 g (4 oz) wholewheat flour
45 ml (3 tbsp) seedless raisins
45 ml (3 tbsp) currants

GLAZE
1 egg white mixed with 10 ml (2 tsp) water

In a large bowl mix water, molasses and honey. When dissolved, sprinkle in the yeast, cover and stand until mixture begins to bubble, about 15 minutes. Stir in coffee, salt, cocoa and butter and when smoothly mixed, add the flours one by one. Mix to a dough, turn on to a lightly floured board and knead vigorously for 10 minutes until smooth and pliable.

Place in a bowl brushed with oil, turn to coat on all sides, then cover bowl with plastic wrap, leaving plenty of room for air and rising. Leave the dough in a warm place until nearly trebled in bulk, about 2-2½ hours. To test, prod with one finger and if the indentation remains, it is ready.

Punch down, add raisins and currants and knead hard for 5 minutes. Shape into a large round, place on oiled baking tray which has been dusted with corn-flour, cover lightly and leave to rise for 1½-2 hours, until doubled. Brush with glaze and bake at 200˚C (400˚F, gas 6) for 50-60 minutes. The bread will be dark and shiny, and should sound hollow when rapped on the bottom. Cool on a wire rack and cut into thin slices.
Makes 1 large loaf

Wholewheat Nut, Raisin and Yoghurt Bread, a superb, nutritious snack-time loaf to serve with cheese, cold meats or pâté.

CARAWAY RYE LOAF

Good with cheese, cold meats, mustard and pickles.

25 ml (5 tsp) molasses
200 ml (7 fl oz) warm water
10 ml (2 tsp) dried yeast
125 g (4 oz) white bread flour
125 g (4 oz) wholewheat flour
150 g (5 oz) rye flour
5 ml (1 tsp) salt
25 ml (5 tsp) oil
5 ml (1 tsp) caraway seeds

Dissolve molasses in water. Sprinkle in yeast, cover and leave to froth. Meanwhile mix remaining ingredients except caraway seeds. Stir bubbly yeast and pour into well in centre of dry ingredients. Mix to a dough. You might have to add about 10 ml (2 tsp) extra warm water. Turn on to a lightly floured board and knead for 10 minutes until smooth. The dough will be firm, rather than spongy. Brush a bowl with oil and turn the ball of dough round in it until coated, then cover and leave to rise for about 1½ hours until doubled.

Punch down and knead in caraway seeds until well distributed. Shape into a 23-cm (9-in) long baton, and place on an oiled baking tray. Make three deep diagonal slashes on the top, then cover loosely with oiled plastic wrap and leave to rise for about 45 minutes or until doubled – the dough will 'fatten' up by rising both upwards and sideways. Either brush top with milk and sprinkle with extra caraway seeds, or sift over a little rye flour. Bake on middle shelf of oven at 200°C (400°F, gas 6) for 10 minutes and then at 180°C (350°F, gas 4) for 25-30 minutes. Turn on to a wire rack to cool.
Makes 1 loaf

NOTE
● *Doughs containing rye flour are always a little sticky.*
● *If bread dough has risen before the oven is ready, immediately remove to a cool place and uncover.*

CHEESE, ONION AND GARLIC BATTER BREAD

10 ml (2 tsp) instant dry yeast
185 g (6½ oz) white bread flour
185 g (6½ oz) wholewheat flour
5 ml (1 tsp) salt
10 ml (2 tsp) caster sugar
2 cloves garlic, crushed
45 g (1½ oz) finely grated Cheddar cheese
1 small onion, finely chopped
45 ml (3 tbsp) chopped parsley
30 g (1 oz) butter
about 350 ml (12 fl oz) warm water
sesame seeds

Mix yeast, both flours, salt, sugar, garlic, cheese, onion and parsley. Rub in butter. Stir in water, using just enough to make a thick, porridge-like batter. Turn the batter into an oiled, 20 x 10 x 6-cm (8 x 4 x 2½-in) loaf tin, sprinkle with sesame seeds, and drape a piece of oiled plastic wrap very lightly over the top. Leave in a warm place for about 30 minutes or until doubled. Bake at 200°C (400°F, gas 6) for 30 minutes and then again at 180°C (350°F, gas 4) for 30 minutes. When the loaf is sufficiently browned, cover lightly with a sheet of greaseproof paper. Stand for a few minutes, turn out, and then return to oven, upside down, for 5 minutes to crisp the sides. Cool on a wire rack.
Makes 1 loaf

INSTANT WHOLEWHEAT BATTER BREAD

The perfect bread for reluctant bakers.

375 g (13 oz) wholewheat flour
125 g (4 oz) white bread flour
60 g (2 oz) crushed wheat
10 ml (2 tsp) instant dry yeast
5 ml (1 tsp) salt
45 g (1½ oz) sunflower seeds
25 ml (5 tsp) oil
25 ml (5 tsp) honey
about 450 ml (¾ pint) warm water
extra sunflower seeds

Mix dry ingredients. Mix in oil and honey. Add 300 ml (½ pint) of the water, then stir in just enough of remaining water to make a soft, sticky dough. Mix well, then turn into an oiled, 23 x 13 x 7.5-cm (9 x 5 x 3-in) loaf tin, sprinkle with sunflower seeds, pressing in lightly, and leave to rise in a warm place until 1-2 cm (½-¾ in) over top of tin. Cover, if you like, with a large plastic bag, allowing it to balloon over the top so that it does not stick to the rising dough. Bake on middle shelf of oven at 200°C (400°F, gas 6) for 30 minutes and then at 180°C (350°F, gas 4) for 20 minutes. Cool on a wire rack.
Makes 1 medium loaf

FOUR-SEED BATTER BREAD

This loaf slices well.

25 ml (5 tsp) honey
550 ml (18 fl oz) warm water
15 ml (1 tbsp) dried yeast
500 g (18 oz) wholewheat flour
125 g (4 oz) white bread flour
45 ml (3 tbsp) sesame seeds
45 g (1½ oz) sunflower seeds
45 ml (3 tbsp) linseeds
5 ml (1 tsp) salt
poppy seeds

Mix honey into 250 ml (8 fl oz) of the warm water and stir to dissolve. Sprinkle in the yeast, cover and leave to froth. Mix flours, sesame seeds, sunflower seeds, linseeds and salt. Stir risen yeast, pour into a well in centre of flour mixture, stir, then slowly add remaining water, or just enough to make a sticky but quite stiff dough. Pat firmly into an oiled, 23 x 13 x 7.5-cm (9 x 5 x 3-in) loaf tin, sprinkle with poppy seeds and leave to rise in a warm place for 1 hour, or until just over the top of the tin. Bake at 200°C (400°F, gas 6) for 30 minutes, and then at 180°C (350°F, gas 4) for 30 minutes. Run a knife round the sides and leave in tin for 1 minute before turning out on to a wire rack to cool.
Makes 1 loaf

OAT BATTER BREAD WITH HERBS

about 375 ml (13 fl oz) warm water
5 ml (1 tsp) caster sugar
10 ml (2 tsp) dried yeast
200 g (7 oz) wholewheat flour
100 g (3½ oz) white bread flour
125 g (4 oz) crushed wheat
90 g (3 oz) rolled oats
5 ml (1 tsp) salt
3-4 cloves garlic, crushed
25 ml (5 tsp) finely chopped fresh
rosemary needles
25 ml (5 tsp) oil
25 ml (5 tsp) honey

Stir sugar into 250 ml (8 fl oz) of the water, sprinkle in the yeast, cover and leave to froth, about 15 minutes. Mix flours, crushed wheat, oats, salt, garlic and rosemary. Stir oil and honey into yeast mixture, then add to flour mixture. Mix, then slowly stir in remaining water, or enough to make a sloppy dough. When well combined, turn into an oiled, 20 x 10 x 6-cm (8 x 4 x 2½-in) loaf tin. Smooth the top, then leave in a warm place until 1 cm (½ in) over the top of the tin – about 45 minutes. Bake at 200°C (400°F, gas 6) for 30 minutes, then at 180°C (350°F, gas 4) for 20-25 minutes. Stand for 1 minute, run a knife round the edges and turn out on to a wire rack to cool. Brush top with melted butter.
Makes 1 loaf

NUTTY WHOLEWHEAT BATTER BREAD

Excellent with pâtés or cheese.

500-600 ml (17-20 fl oz) warm water
15 ml (1 tbsp) honey
10 ml (2 tsp) dried yeast
500 g (18 oz) wholewheat flour
125 g (4 oz) white bread flour
7.5 ml (1½ tsp) salt
15 ml (1 tbsp) oil
45 g (1½ oz) sunflower seeds
60 g (2 oz) linseeds
extra sunflower seeds

A crunchy slice of Instant Wholewheat Batter Bread or Nutty Wholewheat Batter Bread goes well with a crisp salad.

Mix 250 ml (8 fl oz) of the water with the honey and stir until dissolved. Sprinkle yeast on top, cover and leave until frothy, about 10 minutes. Mix wholewheat and white flours, salt and oil. Stir in yeast mixture, sunflower and linseeds. Add rest of water, or just enough to make a soft dough. Spoon into an oiled and floured 20 x 13 x 7.5-cm (8 x 5 x 3-in) loaf tin, patting in firmly. Sprinkle the top with extra sunflower seeds and leave to rise in a warm place for about l hour, or until dough rises to 2 cm (¾ in) above the top of the tin. Bake at 200°C (400°F, gas 6) for 45 minutes. Run a knife round the edges, turn out and cool on a wire rack.
Makes 1 fairly large loaf

ROLLS
& RUSKS

WHITE ROLLS

10 ml (2 tsp) caster sugar
125 ml (4 fl oz) warm water
10 ml (2 tsp) dried yeast
125 ml (4 fl oz) milk
15 g (½ oz) butter
500 g (18 oz) plain flour
5 ml (1 tsp) salt
1 egg, beaten

Stir sugar into water, sprinkle in yeast, cover and leave to froth. Scald milk, add butter and leave until lukewarm. Sift flour and salt together. Stir yeast, pour into well in centre of flour, and mix. Beat egg into cooled milk mixture and add all at once to flour mixture. Mix to a kneadable dough, adding about 25 ml (5 tsp) extra warm water if necessary. Turn on to lightly floured board and knead for 10 minutes until pliable and smooth. Shape into a ball, put back in oiled bowl, turn to coat, cover and leave to rise for 1-1½ hours until doubled.

Punch down, cover and leave to rest for 5-10 minutes. Shape as required. Place on an oiled baking tray and leave to prove for 30-40 minutes until virtually doubled. Brush with milk, sprinkle with suggested toppings, and bake just above the centre of oven at 220°C (425°F, gas 7) for 10 minutes, then at 180°C (350°F, gas 4) for 5 minutes. (Brushing with milk provides a light golden colour; egg-wash may be used, but be careful of over-browning.)
Makes 12 large rolls

Rolls
Roll into balls. Brush with milk and sprinkle with poppy or sesame seeds before baking.

FROM THE BACK: *Baking Powder Rolls; Quick Cheese Crescents; White Rolls in three different shapes.*

Knots
Tie 30-cm (12-in) long sausages of dough into loose knots.

Clover Leaf Rolls
Pinch off pieces of dough, divide into three and form into small balls. Push together to join. May also be dropped into muffin tins.

Cottage Rolls
Pinch off pieces of dough and divide each piece into two-thirds and one-third. Roll the larger pieces into rounds, place on oiled tray and brush with milk, then roll the smaller pieces into balls and place on top. Dip your finger into flour and push right through the two balls.

Bridge Rolls
Shape dough into small sausages and place close together on tray. Before baking, sift flour over the tops. Break apart once baked.

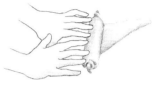

Crescents
Roll a piece of dough into a circle and cut into triangles. Roll up from long end and twist into crescent shapes.

Plaits
Pinch off pieces and divide each into three. Roll into 20-cm (8-in) long sausages. Plait. Brush with milk and sprinkle with sesame seeds before baking.

VARIATION
Rosemary Rolls
For a different flavour, add a large sprig of finely chopped rosemary needles to the flour, and before baking brush tops of rolls with milk and sprinkle with crushed dried rosemary.

CROISSANTS

10 ml (2 tsp) caster sugar
45 ml (3 tbsp) warm water
15 ml (1 tbsp) dried yeast
125 ml (4 fl oz) milk
125 ml (4 fl oz) water
1 egg, separated
400 g (14 oz) plain flour
5 ml (1 tsp) salt
200 g (7 oz) butter
egg white, or an extra yolk beaten
with 5 ml (1 tsp) water

Stir sugar into 45 ml (3 tbsp) water, sprinkle in yeast, cover and leave to froth. Scald milk and water, then leave until lukewarm. Beat egg yolk, then stir in cooled milk-water. Stir yeast and add. Sift 100 g (3½ oz) of the flour with the salt and add. Beat to combine, using a wooden spoon, then give a quick whisk with an egg beater to smooth out lumps. Sift remaining flour and, using two knives, or your fingertips, cut or rub in butter until particles are the size of peas. Pour liquid into a well in the centre, and mix lightly with a wooden spoon until flour is thoroughly moistened and sticky. Push together with a spatula, cover with a damp cloth, and leave to rise in a warm place until doubled – about 1¼ hours – then refrigerate, covered, until well chilled, 1½-2 hours.

Turn on to floured board and knead very lightly with floured fingertips for a few minutes, until smooth. Cut dough into three portions and, using a floured rolling pin, roll each into a 25-30-cm (10-12-in) diameter circle. Cut across into six or eight triangles. Starting at the wide outer edge, roll each triangle inwards. Place, with points facing down, on oiled baking trays. It is important to allow plenty of room for rising and spreading. Twist slightly into crescent shapes, cover loosely with lightly oiled plastic wrap and leave to rise until doubled, about 45 minutes. The tops may be brushed with reserved egg white, but egg-wash gives a better, golden colour. Bake just above centre of oven at 220°C (425°F, gas 7) for 15 minutes. Serve hot, with butter or jam. *Makes 18-24*

VARIATIONS
Chocolate croissants
After cutting the triangle of dough, place two squares of plain chocolate spaced slightly apart, along wide outer edge, then roll up as usual.

Wholewheat croissants
Make as above, except for the following changes: Use 100 ml (3½ oz) warm water instead of 45 ml (3 tbsp), and 125 g (4 oz) plain flour and 250 g (9 oz) wholewheat flour. Sift the plain flour with the salt and add to the milk-water mixture. Whisk as before. Place wholewheat flour into a bowl and rub or cut in butter. Then proceed with the mixing and chilling as above. After cutting and shaping, the dough will need a slightly longer proving period until croissants have doubled. Brush with egg-wash and bake as for white croissants.

MUFFIN TIN WHOLEWHEAT ROLLS

A basic wholewheat batter is used for these wholesome, quickly made muffin-shaped 'rolls'.

500-550 ml (17-18 fl oz) warm water
pinch of caster sugar
10 ml (2 tsp) dried yeast
375 g (13 oz) wholewheat flour
125 g (4 oz) white bread flour
75-150 g (2½-5 oz) seedless raisins (optional)
30 g (1 oz) rolled oats
5 ml (1 tsp) salt
25 ml (5 tsp) oil
25 ml (5 tsp) honey or half honey, half molasses
60 g (2 oz) sunflower seeds
extra sunflower or sesame seeds or crushed wheat

Mix 250 ml (8 fl oz) of the water with a pinch of sugar, sprinkle in yeast, cover and leave to froth. Mix remaining ingredients, exept sunflower or sesame seeds and crushed wheat, in large bowl. Stir yeast and pour into well in centre of dry ingredients. Mix, and then slowly stir in remaining warm water, or just enough to make a thick, moist dough. Spoon into large, oiled muffin tins – they should be just over halfway filled with batter. Top with extra sunflower or sesame seeds, or crushed wheat, pressing in lightly. Cover tin lightly with oiled plastic wrap and leave to rise in a warm place until batter rises, slightly humped, to just over the tops of the tins – about 50-60 minutes. Bake just above centre of oven at 200°C (400°F, gas 6) for about 25 minutes until browned and firm. Stand for a few minutes and then run a knife round the edges to loosen. Cool on a wire rack, and eat freshly baked. *Makes 14-16 large rolls*

BAKING POWDER ROLLS

Although baking powder rolls are not as light as yeast rolls, they are really useful when time is short, and delicious served freshly baked. The dough may be shaped into round balls, plaits, finger rolls or crescents, but this version is particularly crusty.

250 g (9 oz) plain flour
2.5 ml (½ tsp) salt
20 ml (4 tsp) baking powder
10 ml (2 tsp) caster sugar
100 ml (3½ fl oz) milk
100 ml (3½ fl oz) water
15 g (½ oz) butter
extra soft butter, milk and poppy seeds

Sift the flour, salt and baking powder together. Add the sugar. Gently heat the milk, water and butter together, just until butter has melted. Add to dry ingredients. Mix quickly to a soft dough, pat out 1-cm (½-in) thick on floured board, and cut into rounds, using a 7.5-cm (3-in) cutter. Make a dent down the centre of each, using the back of a knife. Spread with a little soft butter, and then fold one half over the other. Brush with milk and sprinkle with poppy seeds. Place on oiled baking tray, cover with a cloth and stand for 5 minutes, then bake just above centre of oven at 220°C (425°F, gas 7) for 15-20 minutes, depending on size of rolls. *Makes about 10*

FETA CHEESE AND GARLIC ROLLS

Beautiful little parcels, with a surprise in the middle. It may be gently reheated if made in advance.

about 350 ml (12 fl oz) warm water
5 ml (1 tsp) caster sugar
10 ml (2 tsp) dried yeast
500 g (18 oz) plain flour
5 ml (1 tsp) salt
20 ml (4 tsp) melted butter
200 g (7 oz) feta cheese
10 ml (2 tsp) dried oregano
4 cloves garlic, crushed
beaten egg and milled black pepper

Stir sugar into 125 ml (4 fl oz) water, sprinkle in yeast, cover and leave to froth. Sift flour and salt. Stir yeast and pour into well in centre of flour. Mix, then add remaining water, or enough to make a workable dough. Knead for 10 minutes on a floured board until creamy and smooth. Shape into a ball, brush a bowl with oil, turn dough round in bowl to coat, then cover and leave to rise for 1¼ hours or until doubled.

Punch down, cover and leave to rest for 5 minutes. Roll out thinly on floured surface. Spread with butter and cut into 16 squares. Cut feta into 16 cubes and toss with oregano and garlic until coated. Place one cube in centre of each square of dough, fold corners to the centre and pinch points tightly to seal. Place on oiled baking trays and cover loosely with oiled plastic wrap. Leave until well risen, about 1 hour. Brush with egg, and grind black pepper over the tops. Bake just above the centre of the oven at 220°C (425°F, gas 7) for 15 minutes. Serve hot.
Makes 16

> **HINT**
> ● *If bread dough does not rise, it is usually because the liquid added was either too hot or too cold. Yeast is 'tougher' than one thinks – the liquid should be warmer than lukewarm.*

Slab Rusks (page 53); Wholewheat Rusks (page 52).

QUICK CHEESE CRESCENTS

375 g (13 oz) plain flour
15 ml (1 tbsp) baking powder
5 ml (1 tsp) salt
5 ml (1 tsp) dry mustard
5 ml (1 tsp) caster sugar
30 g (1 oz) butter
75 g (2½ oz) finely grated, mature
Cheddar cheese
150 ml (¼ pint) milk
150 ml (¼ pint) water

TOPPING
melted butter
45 ml (3 tbsp) grated Cheddar cheese
or
15 ml (1 tbsp) grated Parmesan cheese
paprika

Sift flour, baking powder, salt and mustard together. Add sugar and rub in butter. Mix in the cheese. Mix milk with water and add, mixing quickly and lightly to make a soft but rollable dough. Divide into two, and roll out thinly on a lightly floured board into two 30-cm (12-in) diameter circles. Cut each circle across into eight triangles. Roll up each triangle from the long side towards the point. Curve the dough slightly into horseshoe shapes and arrange on floured baking trays. Bake just above the centre of the oven at 200°C (400°F, gas 6) for 15 minutes. Remove from the oven and brush with melted butter, then sprinkle with Cheddar or Parmesan cheese, as preferred, and lightly dust with paprika. Return to the oven and bake for another 5 minutes.
Makes 16

PITA BREADS

Much experimenting has resulted in what are, to my mind, quite the best of home-made pitas. The shaping is quite different from that of ordinary bread rolls; they rise in the oven like fat little cushions, and form perfect pockets for stuffing. A high baking temperature is important, and to ensure the formation of pockets, the dough should not be creased when rolling, or pinched when turned over just prior to baking.

10 ml (2 tsp) caster sugar
300 ml (½ pint) warm water
10 ml (2 tsp) dried yeast
500 g (18 oz) plain flour
5 ml (1 tsp) salt
30 ml (2 tbsp) oil

Stir sugar into water. Sprinkle in yeast, cover and leave to froth. Sift flour and salt into large bowl. Add oil. Stir bubbly yeast and pour into well in centre of dry ingredients. Combine using a wooden spoon, and then mix with your hands, adding about 30 ml (2 tbsp) extra water, or enough to make a kneadable dough. Turn on to lightly floured board and knead well for 10 minutes until it forms a pliable ball. Return to bowl, brush top with oil, cover and rise for about 1 hour or until doubled.

Punch down and pinch off ten equal pieces. Roll into balls, rest for 5 minutes, and then, using a rolling pin, roll into thin ovals. Place on ungreased baking trays dusted with plain flour. Leave to prove, uncovered, for about 30 minutes, until puffy and doubled in thickness. Turn over carefully and sift a little flour over the tops. Bake, one tray at a time, just above centre of oven at 240°C (475°F, gas 9) for 7 minutes. Remove and wrap in a cloth to soften. Cut a small slice off the edge and press sides gently to open out the pockets.
Makes 10

VARIATION
Wholewheat pitas
Use equal quantities of white bread flour and wholewheat flour. Sift white flour with salt, add wholewheat flour, then proceed as for white pitas. A little extra water may be necessary, but the proving times are about the same.

WHOLEWHEAT RUSKS

Wholesome rusks, delicious for dunking.

1 kg (2¼ lb) wholewheat flour
250 g (9 oz) white bread flour
225 g (8 oz) caster sugar
5 ml (1 tsp) salt
10 ml (2 tsp) baking powder
5 ml (1 tsp) bicarbonate of soda
5 ml (1 tsp) cream of tartar
250 g (9 oz) butter, melted
125 g (4 oz) seedless raisins
500 ml (17 fl oz) buttermilk
2 eggs
200 ml (7 fl oz) oil

In a large bowl mix flours, sugar, salt, baking powder, bicarbonate of soda and cream of tartar. Stir in butter and raisins. Beat buttermilk, eggs and oil. Stir into dry mixture, and knead into a dough. Roll into balls about twice the size of a golf ball. Pack closely into two base-lined and oiled, 20 x 13 x 7.5-cm (8 x 5 x 3-in) loaf tins. Bake at 180°C (350°F, gas 4) for 1 hour. Turn out and leave until cool enough to handle, then break apart, nick in half, and then carefully break again – use a knife to help, but rusks should always be broken, never sliced. Arrange loosely on flat baking trays and dry out at 120-140°C (250-275°F, gas ½-1). They taste even better if allowed to toast slightly.
Makes about 72

Pita Breads form perfect pockets for stuffing with cheese, cold meats or salad.

Bran Flake Buttermilk Rusks

500 g (18 oz) self-raising flour
5 ml (1 tsp) salt
5 ml (1 tsp) baking powder
100 g (3½ oz) caster sugar
75 g (2½ oz) bran flakes
60 g (2 oz) seedless raisins
125 g (4 oz) butter, melted
1 egg
250 ml (8 fl oz) buttermilk
45 ml (3 tbsp) oil

Sift flour, salt and baking powder. Add sugar, bran flakes and raisins. Mix in butter. Beat egg, buttermilk and oil together and add all at once to flour mixture. Mix to soft dough, then knead well until raisins are incorporated and dough forms a ball, leaving sides of mixing bowl clean. Pinch off pieces and roll into 16 balls. Place close together in an oiled and base-lined 23 x 13 x 7.5-cm (9 x 5 x 3-in) loaf tin and bake at 180°C (350°F, gas 4) for 1 hour. When tops are browned, after about 40 minutes, cover with a sheet of greaseproof paper. When cooked, turn out and leave until cool before breaking apart with the help of a sharp knife. Nick the tops and bottoms with a sharp knife and carefully break into two. Place on baking trays and dry out at 110°C (225°F, gas ¼) or in a warming drawer until crisp.
Makes 32

Aniseed Milk Rusks

Light, white rusks which rise like cumulus clouds.

250 ml (8 fl oz) milk
125 ml (4 fl oz) water
125 g (4 oz) butter
100 g (3½ oz) caster sugar
25 ml (5 tsp) oil
1 egg, beaten
5 ml (1 tsp) brown vinegar
1 kg (2¼ lb) self-raising flour
5 ml (1 tsp) cream of tartar
5 ml (1 tsp) salt
5 ml (1 tsp) aniseed

Put milk, water, butter and sugar into a saucepan and heat while stirring, just until sugar has dissolved and butter has melted. Do not overheat. Remove from hob and add oil, egg and vinegar. Sift flour, cream of tartar and salt. Stir in the warm milk mixture and mix to a dough, adding a dash of water if necessary. Add aniseed and knead to a smooth and pliable dough. Shape into balls, about twice the size of a golf ball, and pack closely together into one large or two small oiled and base-lined loaf tins.

Bake for 15 minutes at 200°C (400°F, gas 6), then at 180°C (350°F, gas 4) for a further 45-60 minutes, depending on size of tin used. Place a sheet of greaseproof paper over the top when sufficiently browned. When cooked, turn out, break apart and then nick and break each ball into three or four long rusks. Arrange on baking trays and dry out at 110°C (225°F, gas ¼).
Makes about 36

Buttermilk Rusks

These can also be enjoyed as a delicious type of scone: turn the just-baked bun-loaf out, break apart and serve hot with butter and honey.

1.5 kg (3¼ lb) self-raising flour
10 ml (2 tsp) salt
200 g (7 oz) caster sugar
375 g (13 oz) butter
500 ml (17 fl oz) buttermilk
3 eggs

Mix flour, salt and sugar in a large mixing bowl. Rub in the butter (if in a hurry, this may be melted instead). Mix well. Beat buttermilk with eggs and add. Knead well – the more you knead, the higher they'll rise. If the dough seems a little dry, rinse the buttermilk carton with a little water and add to the mixture to make a medium-soft but never slippery dough. Continue kneading until the dough forms a ball and leaves the sides of the bowl clean, then roll into balls about twice the size of golf balls and pack them closely into two base-lined, oiled and floured 23 x 13 x 7.5-cm

(9 x 5 x 3-in) loaf tins. Bake at 200°C (400°F, gas 6) for 30 minutes, then reduce heat to 180°C (350°F, gas 4) and bake for a further 30 minutes. Turn out and break apart and then, with the help of a knife, break into rusks. Arrange the rusks in single layers on baking trays and dry out at 120°C (250°F, gas ½) or in a warming drawer.
Makes 84-96

Slab Rusks

Definately the easiest rusks to make – the dough is simply patted out flat into a large Swiss roll tin, cut into fingers and baked.

500 g (18 oz) white bread flour
5 ml (1 tsp) salt
10 ml (2 tsp) cream of tartar
5 ml (1 tsp) bicarbonate of soda
100 g (3½ oz) caster sugar
125 g (4 oz) butter
1 egg
250 ml (8 fl oz) buttermilk

Sift flour, salt, cream of tartar and bicarbonate of soda. Mix in sugar. Rub in butter with fingertips until finely crumbled. Beat egg with buttermilk, add to flour mixture and combine, first with a wooden spoon and then with the hands until all the flour is gathered up and mixture forms a soft ball. Pat out into an oiled, 33 x 20-cm (13 x 8-in) Swiss roll tin with fairly high sides. Flour hands lightly if necessary and press out evenly, spreading right into the corners. Slice into 11 (13) strips across and 3 strips down, making 33 (39) fingers. Bake just above centre of oven at 200°C (400°F, gas 6) for 30 minutes. Cut through again, then remove and arrange on baking trays. Dry out at 120°C (250°F, gas ½) or in a warming drawer.
Makes 33 (39)

VARIATION
Wholewheat or brown rusks
Sift 250 g (9 oz) white bread flour, salt, cream of tartar and bicarbonate of soda. Add 250 g (9 oz) wholewheat or brown bread flour, then proceed as above.

QUICK BREADS

AMERICAN CORN BREAD

Baked in a square tin, cut into squares and served while hot, it is popular with fried chicken, or at barbecues or brunches. May also be served with jam and butter for tea.

175 g (6 oz) plain flour or white bread flour
5 ml (1 tsp) salt
20 ml (4 tsp) baking powder
10 ml (2 tsp) caster sugar
175 g (6 oz) fine corn meal
1 egg
300 ml (½ pint) milk
45 ml (3 tbsp) oil

Sift flour, salt, baking powder, sugar and corn meal. Whisk together egg, milk and oil. Pour into a well in centre of dry ingredients and mix lightly and quickly, as for muffins. Pour into oiled, 23-cm (9-in) square baking tin, spreading evenly and lightly with a spatula. Bake just above centre of oven at 220°C (425°F, gas 7) for 20 minutes until golden brown. Cut into 16 squares and cool slightly before removing.
Makes 16 squares

BUTTERMILK HERB BREAD

A wonderfully quick loaf with a tantalizing aroma.

500 g (18 oz) self-raising flour
5ml (1 tsp) dried oregano
5ml (1 tsp) dried thyme
5 ml (1 tsp) salt
5ml (1 tsp) caster sugar
100 ml (7 tbsp) finely chopped parsley
2 cloves garlic, crushed
half a bunch spring onions, chopped
500 ml (17 fl oz) buttermilk
45 ml (3 tbsp) water
grated Parmesan cheese and sesame seeds

FROM THE BACK: *Beer Bread; Feta Cheese and Garlic Rolls (page 51); American Corn Bread; Irish Soda Bread (page 56).*

Mix flour, dried herbs, salt, sugar, parsley, garlic and onions. Stir in the buttermilk. Rinse carton with water and add, mixing well to a sticky dough. Spoon into oiled and floured, 20 x 13 x 7.5-cm (8 x 5 x 3-in) loaf tin. Smooth top, and sprinkle with cheese and sesame seeds. Bake at 180°C (350°F, gas 4) for 1 hour. Run a knife round the sides and turn out on to a wire rack. Cool slightly. Serve freshly baked, with butter.
Makes 1 loaf

SAVOURY CHEESE SODA BREAD

The unusual combination of onion, carrot, herbs and cheese makes an aromatic, golden-brown loaf – a marvellous variation on the Irish soda bread theme.

125 g (4 oz) white bread flour
2.5 ml (½ tsp) salt
2.5 ml (½ tsp) bicarbonate of soda
2.5 ml (½ tsp) cream of tartar
125 g (4 oz) brown bread flour
15 g (½ oz) butter
1 medium onion, coarsely grated
90 g (3 oz) coarsely grated carrot
2.5 ml (½ tsp) mixed dried herbs
45 ml (3 tbsp) chopped parsley
45 g (1½ oz) finely grated Cheddar cheese
about 200 ml (7 fl oz) buttermilk
milk and extra cheese or sesame seeds

Sift white bread flour, salt, bicarbonate of soda and cream of tartar. Mix in brown flour and rub in butter. Mix in onion, carrot, herbs, parsley and cheese. Add just enough buttermilk to form a soft dough. Mix lightly and then pat and toss mixture together to shape into a round. Place on floured baking tray and, using the back of a knife, score deeply into eight triangles. Brush with milk and sprinkle with extra cheese or sesame seeds. Bake on middle shelf of oven at 200°C (400°F, gas 6) for 30 minutes. Transfer to a wire rack, but serve very fresh, broken into triangles.
Makes 1 round loaf

BAKING POWDER BREAD

500 g (18 oz) white bread flour
20 ml (4 tsp) baking powder
5 ml (1 tsp) salt
10 ml (2 tsp) caster sugar
45 g (1½ oz) butter
175 ml (6 fl oz) milk
175 ml (6 fl oz) water

Sift flour, baking powder and salt. Add sugar. Rub in butter until finely crumbled. Mix milk and water and add, mixing quickly to a soft dough. You might have to add about 10 ml (2 tsp) extra water. Do not knead, but pat it about until it holds together, then pat out flat into a rectangle and roll up like a Swiss roll. Place, join side down, in an oiled, 20 x 10 x 6-cm (8 x 4 x 2½-in) loaf tin. Brush with milk and bake towards the top of the oven at 220°C (425°F, gas 7) for 45 minutes until a golden brown. Turn out on to a wire rack and cool.
Makes 1 loaf

BEER BREAD

Add chopped mixed fresh herbs, crushed garlic or cheese for a change.

375 g (13 oz) self-raising flour
125 g (4 oz) wholewheat flour
2.5 ml (½ tsp) salt
10 ml (2 tsp) caster sugar
75 ml (5 tbsp) finely chopped parsley
340 ml (11½ oz) bottled beer (unchilled)
sesame seeds

Mix dry ingredients, including parsley. Stir in beer, and mix well to a tacky, springy dough. Turn into oiled and base-lined 20 x 10 x 6-cm (8 x 4 x 2½-in) loaf tin, level top and sprinkle with sesame seeds. Bake at 180°C (350°F, gas 4) for 1 hour 10 minutes, turn out on to wire rack, remove lining paper and cool. This loaf will not be browned when cooked, but rises well and has a crisp, humped crust. Any leftovers are good toasted.
Makes 1 loaf

IRISH SODA BREAD

My favourite version of this bread, with none of that overt taste of bicarbonate. Quantities are easily doubled to make one large or two small rounds.

125 g (4 oz) white bread flour
125 g (4 oz) plain flour
2.5 ml (½ tsp) salt
2.5 ml (½ tsp) bicarbonate of soda
2.5 ml (½ tsp) cream of tartar
15 g (½ oz) butter
225-250 ml (7½-8 fl oz) buttermilk
beaten egg

Sift flours with salt, bicarbonate of soda and cream of tartar. Rub in butter. Add 225 ml (7½ fl oz) buttermilk all at once and mix quickly to make a soft dough, adding the extra 25 ml (5 tsp) only if further moistening is necessary. Turn on to floured board and shape into a 15-cm (6-in) diameter cake. Place on floured baking tray and score top deeply into quarters, using the back of a knife. Brush with beaten egg and bake on middle shelf of oven at 200°C (400°F, gas 6) for 30 minutes. Serve freshly baked.
Makes 1 loaf

CHEESE, ONION AND NUT BREAD

This is a super, fairly dense and crunchy savoury loaf which takes only a few minutes to mix.

375 g (13 oz) self-raising flour
30 g (1 oz) untoasted wheat germ
5 ml (1 tsp) salt
5ml (1 tsp) caster sugar
3 cloves garlic, crushed
1 medium onion, coarsely grated
100 g (3½ oz) finely grated Cheddar cheese
60 g (2 oz) finely chopped toasted walnuts or pecan nuts
250 ml (8 fl oz) buttermilk
125 ml (4 fl oz) water
paprika

Mix flour, wheat germ, salt, sugar, garlic, onion, cheese and nuts. Stir in buttermilk and water and mix to a thick and sticky batter. Turn batter into an oiled, 20 x 13 x 7.5-cm (8 x 5 x 3-in) loaf tin and level top with a spatula. Sprinkle with paprika and bake on middle shelf of oven at 180°C (350°F, gas 4) for 1 hour. Turn out and cool on a wire rack.
Makes 1 medium loaf

PLAIN BAKING POWDER COB

Makes one small, crusty cob – a most useful quick-bread, and delicious served freshly baked.

185 g (6½ oz) plain flour
2.5 ml (½ tsp) salt
20 ml (4 tsp) baking powder
125 g (4 oz) wholewheat flour
200 ml (7 fl oz) milk
1 egg
extra flour or milk and poppy seeds

Sift plain flour, salt and baking powder. Add wholewheat flour. Beat milk and egg and add. Mix to a dough, and knead lightly until it holds together. Pat into a 15-cm (6-in) diameter cake and place on floured baking tray. Make three diagonal slashes across the top, and sift over a little flour, or brush with milk and sprinkle with poppy seeds. Bake just above centre of oven at 220°C (425°F, gas 7) for 20-25 minutes. Transfer to a wire rack. Break into chunks to serve.
Makes 1 small loaf

BUTTERMILK SCONE BREAD

Serve this delicious, quickly made bread, broken into chunks, with butter and marmalade for a leisurely Sunday breakfast.

500 g (18 oz) self-raising flour
5 ml (1 tsp) salt
15 ml (1 tbsp) caster sugar
30 g (1 oz) butter
about 425 ml (14½ fl oz) buttermilk
milk, sesame and poppy seeds

Sift flour with salt. Add sugar and rub in butter. Make a well in the centre of the flour mixture and pour in enough buttermilk to make a soft dough. Turn out on to floured board and knead very lightly while patting out to a 20-cm (8-in) round, rather like a giant scone. Place on oiled baking tray and cut a fairly deep cross on the top. Brush each quarter with milk and then sprinkle alternate quarters with sesame and poppy seeds. Bake on middle shelf of oven at 220°C (425°F, gas 7) for 10 minutes, then reduce heat to 180°C (350°F, gas 4) and bake for a further 30 minutes.
Makes 1 round loaf

> **NOTE**
> ● *Wholewheat and white flours can often be interchanged; however wholewheat flour will need more liquid.*

BABY MARROW TEA LOAF

A large, spicy loaf that is delicious served sliced and buttered.

3 eggs
250 ml (8 fl oz) oil
200 g (7 oz) caster sugar
few drops vanilla essence
300 g (11 oz) baby marrows
250 g (9 oz) plain flour (half brown
bread flour may be used)
5 ml (1 tsp) bicarbonate of soda
5 ml (1 tsp) baking powder
2.5 ml (½ tsp) salt
5 ml (1 tsp) ground cinnamon
5 ml (1 tsp) ground mixed spice
60-125 g (2-4 oz) chopped pecan nuts
or walnuts

Beat eggs, oil, sugar and vanilla together until light. Trim, pare and coarsely grate raw baby marrows and stir in. Sift dry ingredients together and add. Finally stir in nuts. Mix well and turn into oiled, base-lined and floured 23 x 13 x 7.5-cm (9 x 5 x 3-in) loaf tin. Bake at 180°C (350°F, gas 4) on middle shelf of oven for 1 hour to 1 hour 10 minutes. Cool for 5 minutes, then turn out on to a wire rack, remove lining paper and cool.
Makes 1 loaf

BROWN FRUIT LOAF

250 g (9 oz) mixed dried fruit
200 g (7 oz) demerara sugar
250 ml (8 fl oz) water
45 ml (3 tbsp) oil
1.25 ml (¼ tsp) grated nutmeg
5 ml (1 tsp) ground cinnamon
2.5 ml (½ tsp) ground ginger
1.25 ml (¼ tsp) salt
45 g (1½ oz) chopped walnuts, pecan
or Brazil nuts
125 ml (4 fl oz) natural drinking
yoghurt
1 egg
5 ml (1 tsp) bicarbonate of soda
250 g (9 oz) brown bread flour
5 ml (1 tsp) baking powder
few drops vanilla essence

A Cheese, Onion and Nut Bread slices well. Break an Irish Soda Bread in chunks.

Put dried fruit mixture, sugar, water, oil, spices and salt into a saucepan, bring to the boil and simmer for 5 minutes. Cool thoroughly. Add nuts. Beat yoghurt, egg and bicarbonate of soda together, and add to fruit mixture alternately with flour. Finally add baking powder and vanilla. Spoon into an oiled and floured, 20 x 10 x 6-cm (8 x 4 x 2½-in) loaf tin and smooth top with the back of a spoon dipped into hot water. Bake at 160°C (325°F, gas 3) for about 45 minutes. Turn out and cool on a wire rack.
Makes 1 loaf

COFFEE-GLAZED NUTMEG LOAF

Topped with flavoured glacé icing and attractively decorated, this enticing, spicy loaf looks just as good as it tastes.

250 g (9 oz) plain flour
5 ml (1 tsp) baking powder
10 ml (2 tsp) grated nutmeg
pinch of salt
200 g (7 oz) demerara sugar
125 g (4 oz) soft butter
200 ml (7 fl oz) buttermilk
1 egg
5 ml (1 tsp) bicarbonate of soda
60 g (2 oz) chopped Brazil nuts, lightly toasted
few drops vanilla essence

GLAZE
60 g (2 oz) sifted icing sugar
5 ml (1 tsp) instant coffee granules
10-15 ml (2-3 tsp) water
blanched almonds and cherries to decorate

Sift flour, baking powder, nutmeg and salt. Add sugar, then rub in butter until mixture is like fine breadcrumbs. (A hand-held electric beater is ideal.) Beat buttermilk with egg and bicarbonate of soda. Stir into flour mixture, then add nuts and vanilla. Mix well and turn into oiled and base-lined 20 x 10 x 6-cm (8 x 4 x 2½-in) loaf tin. Spread evenly, smoothing top with the back of a spoon dipped into hot water. Bake at 180°C (350°F, gas 4) for 1 hour. Turn out on to a wire rack, remove lining paper and cool. Turn right side up to glaze.

For the glaze, mix icing sugar, coffee and enough water to make a mixture that will just pour. Glaze top of loaf, allowing it to run down the sides. When set, decorate with almond 'flowers' centred with cherries. Serve sliced, with or without butter.
Makes 1 loaf

FRUIT AND CARROT LOAF

This recipe makes two medium-sized, deliciously moist loaves.

250 g (9 oz) mixed dried fruit
600 ml (1 pint) water
400 g (14 oz) demerara sugar
180 g (6 oz) coarsely grated carrots
30 g (1 oz) butter
10 ml (2 tsp) ground mixed spice
250 g (9 oz) plain flour
10 ml (2 tsp) bicarbonate of soda
10 ml (2 tsp) baking powder
1.25 ml (¼ tsp) salt
250 g (9 oz) wholewheat flour
125 g (4 oz) chopped walnuts or pecan nuts (optional)

Place fruit, water, sugar, carrots, butter and spice in a wide-based saucepan, bring to the boil, cover and simmer for 10 minutes. Cool completely. Sift plain flour with bicarbonate of soda, baking powder and salt and stir into cooled mixture. Mix in wholewheat flour – the batter will be soft. Add nuts, if using. Turn into two oiled and base-lined, or non-stick, 20 x 10 x 6-cm (8 x 4 x 2½-in) loaf tins, and bake at 160°C (325°F, gas 3) for 1 hour. Test with a skewer, and if cooked, remove from oven and allow to stand for 5 minutes before turning on to a wire rack and removing lining paper. Leave to cool.
Makes 2 loaves

DATE LOAF

250 g (9 oz) stoned dates, finely chopped
30 g (1 oz) butter
200 g (7 oz) demerara sugar
2.5 ml (½ tsp) bicarbonate of soda
250 ml (8 fl oz) boiling water
250 g (9 oz) white bread flour (half brown bread flour may be used)
pinch of salt
5 ml (1 tsp) baking powder
few drops vanilla essence
60 g (2 oz) chopped walnuts (optional)

Put dates into a bowl with butter and sugar. Sprinkle with bicarbonate of soda and pour boiling water over. Leave to cool, stirring occasionally. Sift flour, salt and baking powder. Add cooled date mixture. Add vanilla and nuts and mix well. Pour into an oiled and base-lined 20 x 10 x 6-cm (8 x 4 x 2½-in) loaf tin. Level top with the back of a spoon dipped into hot water and bake at 160°C (325°F, gas 3) in the centre of the oven for 1 hour. Turn out on to a wire rack, remove lining paper and cool.
Makes 1 loaf

HINT
● *When measuring honey or syrup, use a measure that has been oiled, or used to measure oil.*

NUTTY DARK GINGERBREAD

Satisfying and pleasantly spicy. Serve sliced and buttered.

200 g (7 oz) demerara sugar
125 g (4 oz) butter
25 ml (5 tsp) syrup or honey
25 ml (5 tsp) molasses
45 ml (3 tbsp) milk
45 ml (3 tbsp) water
125 g (4 oz) brown bread flour
125 g (4 oz) white bread flour
1.25 ml (¼ tsp) salt
1.25 ml (¼ tsp) grated nutmeg
15 ml (1 tbsp) ground ginger
7.5 ml (1½ tsp) baking powder
2.5 ml (½ tsp) bicarbonate of soda
60 g (2 oz) chopped walnuts or pecan nuts
1 egg, beaten

Heat the sugar, butter, syrup or honey, molasses, milk and water gently. Mix remaining ingredients, except egg. Pour hot, melted mixture into dry ingredients and mix well. Stir in egg. The mixture should be soft. Pour into oiled and floured, 20 x 10 x 6-cm (8 x 4 x 2½-in) loaf tin and bake at 180°C (350°F, gas 4) for about 45 minutes.
Makes 1 loaf

SPICED HONEY LOAF

This honey loaf is a large, spicy loaf with coffee to provide the rich brown colour, and a scattering of brandy-soaked fruit. After baking, it may be topped with glacé icing and studded with blanched almonds. Serve sliced and buttered.

150 g (5 oz) mixed dried fruit, including some
glacé cherries
2 large knobs preserved ginger, chopped
25 ml (5 tsp) brandy
375 g (13 oz) plain flour
15 ml (1 tbsp) baking powder
2.5 ml (½ tsp) bicarbonate of soda
1.25 ml (¼ tsp) salt
15 ml (1 tbsp) ground ginger
5 ml (1 tsp) ground cinnamon
large pinch ground cloves
200 g (7 oz) demerara sugar
2 eggs
140 g (4½ oz) golden honey
15 ml (1 tbsp) instant coffee granules
250 ml (8 fl oz) water
125 ml (4 fl oz) oil

Place dried fruit and ginger in small bowl. Add brandy, cover and stand for at least 1 hour. Sift flour, baking powder, bicarbonate of soda, salt and spices. Add sugar. Beat eggs until light, then beat in honey, the coffee dissolved in the water, and the oil. Add to flour mixture and mix well until thoroughly combined. Fold in fruit and turn into base-lined and oiled, 23 x 13 x 7.5-cm (9 x 5 x 3-in) loaf tin. Bake on middle shelf of oven at 180°C (350°F, gas 4) for 1¼ hours. Test with a skewer, then stand for a few minutes before turning out on to a wire rack and removing lining paper. Leave to cool.
Makes 1 very large loaf

HINT
• *Lightly toasting nuts before use brings out the flavour. Chop nuts, then spread them out on a baking trays and place in a moderate oven until lightly browned.*

FROM LEFT TO RIGHT: *Date Loaf; Bran Fruit Loaf; Fruit and Carrot Loaf.*

BRAN FRUIT LOAF

45 g (1½ oz) bran flakes
150 g (5 oz) demerara sugar
150 g (5 oz) mixed dried fruit
250 ml (8 fl oz) milk
60 ml (4 tbsp) oil
185 g (6½ oz) plain flour
15 ml (1 tbsp) baking powder
1.25 ml (¼ tsp) salt
5 ml (1 tsp) ground mixed spice
45 g (1½ oz) finely chopped pecan nuts (optional)
few drops vanilla essence

Place bran flakes, sugar, fruit, milk and oil in large bowl. Stir until combined and then stand for 30 minutes. Sift flour, baking powder, salt and spice. Add to fruit mixture, together with nuts, if using, and vanilla. Mix well, using a wooden spoon. Turn into an oiled and base-lined 20 x 10 x 6-cm (8 x 4 x 2½-in) loaf tin and bake on middle shelf of oven at 180°C (350°F, gas 4) for 1 hour, then test with a skewer. If cooked, stand for a few minutes before turning out on to a wire rack and removing lining paper. Leave to cool.
Makes 1 loaf

Chocolate, Carrot and Ginger Loaf

This is quite different from the ordinary carrot loaf; it is large, dark and economical, with an unusual combination of ingredients. Serve sliced and buttered, rather than iced.

125 g (4 oz) plain flour
45 ml (3 tbsp) cocoa powder
5 ml (1 tsp) ground mixed spice
5 ml (1 tsp) bicarbonate of soda
5 ml (1 tsp) baking powder
pinch of salt
125 g (4 oz) wholewheat flour
125 g (4 oz) seedless raisins
3 knobs preserved ginger, chopped
45 g (1½ oz) desiccated coconut
2 eggs*
200 g (7 oz) demerara sugar
125 ml (4 fl oz) oil
180 g (6 oz) coarsely grated carrots
few drops vanilla essence

Sift the plain flour, cocoa, spice, bicarbonate of soda, baking powder and salt together. Add the wholewheat flour, raisins, ginger and coconut. Beat eggs, sugar and oil. Add to flour mixture, and when combined, stir in carrots and vanilla. Mix to a fairly stiff, sticky batter. Turn into oiled and base-lined 20 x 13 x 7.5-cm (8 x 5 x 3 in) loaf tin, smooth top with the back of a spoon dipped into hot water, and bake on middle shelf of oven at 180°C (350°F, gas 4) for about 1 hour 10 minutes – test with a skewer. Stand for a few minutes before turning out on to a wire rack and removing lining paper. Leave to cool.
Makes 1 loaf

* It is important to use extra large eggs, or batter will be too stiff.

Fruit Tea Loaf

This is just one good version of the ever popular fruit loaf using cold tea.

500 g (18 oz) mixed dried fruit
2 tea bags
500 ml (17 fl oz) boiling water
25 ml (5 tsp) oil
2 eggs, lightly beaten
300 g (11 oz) demerara sugar
500 g (18 oz) self-raising flour
1.25 ml (¼ tsp) salt
5 ml (1 tsp) ground cinnamon
5 ml (1 tsp) ground mixed spice
5 ml (1 tsp) baking powder
few drops vanilla essence

Put fruit and tea bags into bowl. Pour boiling water over, stir and leave overnight. Next day turn mixture into large mixing bowl, remove tea bags, and add oil, eggs and sugar, mixing well. Sift flour, salt, spices and baking powder. Add to fruit mixture, mix well, and stir in vanilla. Turn mixture, which will be thick and sticky, into two oiled and base-lined 20 x 10 x 6-cm (8 x 4 x 2½-in) loaf tins. Level tops with the back of a spoon dipped into hot water. Bake on middle shelf of oven at 180°C (350°F, gas 4) for 1-1¼ hours – test with a skewer to make sure they are cooked through. Turn out on to a wire rack, remove lining paper and leave to cool. Serve sliced and buttered.
Makes 2 loaves

Coconut Yoghurt Loaf

All the measuring is conveniently done in the yoghurt carton for this large, moist loaf.

175 ml (6 fl oz) carton natural Bulgarian yoghurt
1 carton caster sugar
1 carton oil
3 eggs
few drops vanilla essence
3 cartons self-raising flour
2 cartons desiccated coconut

Whisk yoghurt, sugar, oil, eggs and vanilla until thick and creamy. Add flour, one carton at a time, mixing well. Add coconut and mix to a very soft batter. Pour into oiled and base-lined 23 x 13 x 7.5-cm (9 x 5 x 3-in) loaf tin and bake on middle shelf of oven at 160°C (325°F, gas 3) for 1¼ hours. Stand for a few minutes, then turn out on to a wire rack. Remove lining paper and leave to cool.
Makes 1 loaf

Glazed Lemon Loaf

Light, lovely and lemony.

125 g (4 oz) soft butter
150 g (5 oz) caster sugar
finely grated rind of 1 lemon
250 g (9 oz) white bread flour plus
10 ml (2 tsp) extra
10 ml (2 tsp) baking powder
pinch of salt
60 g (2 oz) finely chopped mixed peel
2 eggs
250 ml (8 fl oz) milk
few drops vanilla essence

GLAZE
45 ml (3 tbsp) caster sugar
45 ml (3 tbsp) fresh lemon juice

Cream butter, sugar and lemon rind until light. Sift flour, baking powder and salt. Add mixed peel. Add eggs to creamed mixture, one by one, adding 5 ml (1 tsp) flour with each egg. Fold in flour mixture. Add milk and vanilla. Whisk to a soft batter. Pour into oiled, base-lined 20 x 13 x 7.5-cm (8 x 5 x 3-in) loaf tin and smooth top with back of a spoon dipped into hot water. Bake at 180°C (350°F, gas 4) for 1 hour.

Just before end of baking time, make glaze by mixing caster sugar and lemon juice in small saucepan. Stir over low heat to dissolve sugar and then boil over high heat for 1 minute. Remove baked loaf from oven, prick the top all over with a thin skewer, and slowly drizzle lemon syrup over. Stand in tin until cold, then run a knife round the edges, turn out and remove lining paper.
Makes 1 loaf

FROM THE BACK: *Coconut Yoghurt Loaf; Chocolate Carrot and Ginger Loaf; Glazed Lemon Loaf.*

ONE-BOWL ORANGE LOAF

A great standby when time is at a premium – assemble the ingredients and whip up this loaf for tea in a matter of minutes.

250 g (9 oz) plain flour or white bread flour
150 g (5 oz) caster sugar
10 ml (2 tsp) baking powder
pinch of salt
125 ml (4 fl oz) oil
125 ml (4 fl oz) fresh orange juice
5 ml (1 tsp) finely grated orange rind
2 eggs
few drops vanilla essence

GLAZE
25 ml (5 tsp) orange juice
15 g (½ oz) butter
175 g (6 oz) sifted icing sugar

Sift flour, sugar, baking powder and salt. Add oil, juice and rind. Using an electric beater, mix for 1 minute on medium speed. Add eggs and vanilla. Beat for 45 seconds or just until mixed. Pour into a base-lined, oiled and floured, 20 x 13 x 7.5-cm (8 x 5 x 3-in) loaf tin and bake at 160°C (325°F, gas 3) on middle shelf of oven for 1 hour. Stand for 5 minutes, then turn out, remove lining paper and cool on a wire rack.

To make the glaze, heat orange juice and butter in small saucepan, add icing sugar and stir over very low heat until smooth. Pour over top of cold loaf, allowing glaze to trickle down the sides. Decorate with cherries and angelica.
Makes 1 loaf

HINT
● *Be wary of adding too much water to a batter bread. If you make it to wet, the loaf will deflate in the oven. The consistency should be fairly thick and moist, like a fruit cake mixture.*

One-bowl Orange Loaf; Banana Loaf; Baby Marrow Tea Loaf (page 57).

PUMPKIN, PECAN AND RAISIN LOAF

A spicy, caramel-coloured loaf.

250 g (9 oz) white bread flour
5 ml (1 tsp) baking powder
2.5 ml (½ tsp) salt
5 ml (1 tsp) ground cinnamon
5 ml (1 tsp) ground ginger
large pinch of ground cloves
45 g (1½ oz) finely chopped
pecan nuts
90 g (3 oz) seedless raisins
100 g (3½ oz) soft butter
200 g (7 oz) demerara sugar
2 eggs
375 ml (12 fl oz) smooth pumpkin
purée
5 ml (1 tsp) bicarbonate of soda
25 ml (5 tsp) water

Sift the flour, baking powder, salt and spices together. Add nuts and raisins. Cream butter and sugar. Add eggs singly, beating well. Mix in pumpkin purée, and then add flour mixture. Continue beating until combined. Dissolve bicarbonate of soda in the water and stir into batter. Turn into oiled and base-lined 20 x 13 x 7.5-cm (8 x 5 x 3-in) loaf tin, and bake at 180°C (350°F, gas 4) for 1 hour. Stand for 5 minutes before turning out on to a wire rack and removing lining paper. Leave to cool.
Makes 1 loaf

BANANA LOAF

A reliable old favourite.

250 g (9 oz) white or brown
bread flour
10 ml (2 tsp) baking powder
1.25 ml (¼ tsp) bicarbonate of soda
1.25 ml (¼ tsp) salt
5 ml (1 tsp) ground cinnamon
125 g (4 oz) soft butter
200 g (7 oz) caster sugar
2 eggs
4 large, ripe bananas, mashed
60 g (2 oz) chopped walnuts
few drops vanilla essence

Sift flour, baking powder, bicarbonate of soda, salt and cinnamon together. Cream the butter and sugar until light. Add the eggs singly, beating well between additions and adding 5 ml (1 tsp) of the flour mixture with each egg. Add flour mixture to creamed mixture alternately with bananas, beating well until smooth. Stir in nuts and vanilla. Pour the batter into lightly oiled and base-lined 23 x 13 x 7.5-cm (9 x 5 x 3-in) loaf tin. Smooth top with the back of a spoon dipped into hot water, then bake at 180°C (350°F, gas 4) for 50-60 minutes. Turn out, remove paper and cool. Serve sliced and buttered.
Makes 1 loaf

BUTTERMILK FRUIT LOAF

Economical and easy-to-make, rather like a light slab fruit cake. Serve sliced and buttered.

375 g (13 oz) self-raising flour
5 ml (1 tsp) ground cinnamon
1.25 ml (¼ tsp) grated nutmeg
1.25 ml (¼ tsp) salt
225 g (8 oz) mixed dried fruit
375 ml (12 fl oz) buttermilk
1 egg
45 ml (3 tbsp) honey
75 ml (5 tbsp) caster sugar
100 ml (3½ fl oz) oil
cherries and blanched almonds

Sift the flour, spices and salt together. Mix in fruit. Whisk buttermilk, egg, honey, sugar and oil together. Add to flour mixture and combine lightly but thoroughly. Turn into a base-lined and oiled 23 x 13 x 7.5-cm (9 x 5 x 3-in) loaf tin and level top with back of a spoon dipped into hot water. As the batter is fairly stiff, cherries and almonds may be arranged on the top. Bake on middle shelf of oven at 180°C (350°F, gas 4) for 1 hour. Stand for 1 minute before turning out on to a wire rack and removing lining paper. Leave to cool.
Makes 1 loaf

SURPRISE LOAF

This colourful tea loaf combines two vegetables in a most unusual and delicious way. Serve sliced and buttered.

200 ml (7 fl oz) oil
200 g (7 oz) caster sugar
2 eggs
45 g (1½ oz) sunflower seeds
(preferably toasted)
90 g (3 oz) coarsely grated carrots
90 g (3 oz) peeled and coarsely
grated beetroot
125 g (4 oz) plain flour
2.5 ml (½ tsp) salt
15 ml (1 tbsp) baking powder
5 ml (1 tsp) ground cinnamon
2.5 ml (½ tsp) ground mixed spice
125 g (4 oz) wholewheat flour

Whisk oil and sugar until creamy, then add the eggs and beat well. Mix in sunflower seeds, carrots and beetroot. Sift plain flour, salt, baking powder and spices and add to creamed mixture. Fold in wholewheat flour. Turn into oiled and base-lined 23 x 13 x 7.5-cm (9 x 5 x 3-in) loaf tin and bake at 180°C (350°F, gas 4) for 1 hour. Stand for 1 minute, then turn out on to a wire rack, remove lining paper and cool.
Makes 1 loaf

BASIC MUFFINS

Plain, golden muffins, delicious with butter and cheese, honey or jam.

250 g (9 oz) plain flour
15 ml (1 tbsp) baking powder
1.25 ml (¼ tsp) salt
45 ml (3 tbsp) caster sugar
60 ml (4 tbsp) oil
1 egg, beaten
125 ml (4 fl oz) milk
125 ml (4 fl oz) water

Sift flour, baking powder and salt. Add sugar. Whisk together the oil, egg, milk and water. Pour all at once into well in centre of dry ingredients. Mix lightly and quickly – use a wooden spoon and do not beat. Spoon into oiled muffin tins, making them two-thirds full. Bake at 200°C (400°F, gas 6) for 20-25 minutes. Cool slightly, loosen with a knife and remove. Serve as soon as possible.
Makes about 12

APPLE, RAISIN AND HONEY MUFFINS

125 g (4 oz) white bread flour
5 ml (1 tsp) ground cinnamon
1.25 ml (¼ tsp) grated nutmeg
small pinch of ground cloves
1.25 ml (¼ tsp) salt
15 ml (1 tbsp) baking powder
125 g (4 oz) wholewheat flour
1 egg
45 ml (3 tbsp) oil
125 ml (4 fl oz) water
125 ml (4 fl oz) milk
45 ml (3 tbsp) demerara sugar
45 ml (3 tbsp) honey
2 medium Golden Delicious apples
45 g (1½ oz) seedless raisins

Basic Muffins; Apple, Raisin and Honey Muffins.

Sift white flour, spices, salt and baking powder. Mix in wholewheat flour. Whisk together the egg, oil, water, milk, sugar and honey. Make a well in centre of dry ingredients and pour in the liquid ingredients. Add peeled and coarsely grated apples, and raisins. Stir quickly until just combined – do not beat. Spoon into oiled muffin tins, making them three-quarters full, and bake at 200°C (400°F, gas 6) for 20 minutes. Run a knife round the edges to loosen, and cool on a wire rack. Serve buttered.
Makes 12-14

FAVOURITE FRUIT MUFFINS

Flop-proof, nutritious, sweet and spicy muffins which rise perfectly. They are great for lunch-boxes. Chopped nuts may be added with the sugar, if desired.

250 ml (8 fl oz) boiling water
150 g (5 oz) mixed dried fruit
30 g (1 oz) butter
125 g (4 oz) white bread flour
5 ml (1 tsp) baking powder
5 ml (1 tsp) bicarbonate of soda
1.25 ml (¼ tsp) salt
5 ml (1 tsp) ground mixed spice
2.5 ml (½ tsp) ground cinnamon
125 g (4 oz) wholewheat flour
75 g (2½ oz) demerara sugar
few drops vanilla essence

Pour water over fruit and butter in a bowl and stand for 10 minutes, stirring once to melt butter. Sift white flour, baking powder, bicarbonate of soda, salt and spices. Add wholewheat flour and sugar. Pour fruit mixture into well in centre of dry ingredients and mix together with vanilla until combined – do not overmix. Spoon into oiled muffin tins, making them three-quarters full, and bake at 200°C (400°F, gas 6) for 15-18 minutes until richly browned and firm. Run a knife round the edges to remove and cool on a wire rack. Serve freshly baked, with butter.
Makes 12-14

PROCESSOR HERB MUFFINS

Fragrant with herbs and made in a jiffy, these muffins are splendid served hot from the oven with a bowl of soup. The amount of herbs is approximate – there is no need to count little leaves and sprigs meticulously – let the given quantities merely act as a guide. The important factor is to use fresh herbs.

4 sprigs marjoram
2 sprigs thyme
about 24 rosemary needles
8 large sage leaves
few sprigs parsley
250 g (9 oz) plain flour
15 ml (1 tbsp) baking powder
1.25 ml (¼ tsp) salt
5 ml (1 tsp) caster sugar
1 large clove garlic, chopped
2 spring onions, plus some tops, chopped
1 egg
60 ml (4 tbsp) oil
200 ml (7 fl oz) milk
grated Cheddar cheese

Strip leaves from marjoram and thyme and place in food processor fitted with grinding blade together with the rosemary, sage, parsley, flour, baking powder, salt, sugar, garlic and spring onions. Process until herbs are finely chopped. Tip into mixing bowl. Beat egg with oil and milk. Pour into well in centre of flour mixture and mix very quickly to a soft batter. Pour into well-oiled muffin tins, making them about two-thirds full. Sprinkle with the cheese and bake at 200°C (400°F, gas 6) for 20-25 minutes. Stand for a few seconds and then run a knife round the edges to loosen. Serve hot, with butter.
Makes 12 large muffins

Spring Onion, Cheese and Celery Muffins

Marvellously aromatic, golden-brown, light muffins. Super with soup.

250 g (9 oz) self-raising flour
2.5 ml (½ tsp) dry mustard
1.25 ml (¼ tsp) salt
60 g (2 oz) butter
2 large sticks celery
4 spring onions, plus some
of the tops, chopped
45 g (1½ oz) grated Cheddar cheese
1 egg
250 ml (8 fl oz) buttermilk
paprika

Sift the flour, mustard and salt together. Rub in the butter until finely crumbled. Grate the celery coarsely and squeeze dry with paper towels if necessary. Add to dry mixture together with onions and cheese. Beat egg with buttermilk and add. Mix quickly and lightly. Spoon the batter into oiled muffin tins, making them two-thirds full. Lightly dust with paprika and bake at 200˚C (400˚F, gas 6) for 20-25 minutes. Leave to stand for about 1 minute before removing. Serve warm with butter.
Makes 12-14

Green Pepper and Onion Muffins

Aromatic, savoury muffins.

1 egg
45 ml (3 tbsp) oil
125 g (4 oz) low-fat soft cheese
100 ml (3½ fl oz) milk
100 ml (3½ fl oz) water
250 g (9 oz) plain flour
15 ml (1 tbsp) baking powder
2.5 ml (½ tsp) salt
60 ml (4 tbsp) finely chopped green
pepper (discard all seeds and ribs)
6 spring onions, chopped
2.5 ml (½ tsp) mixed dried herbs
12-16 small cubes of Gouda cheese

Beat the egg, oil, soft cheese, milk and water together. Sift flour, baking powder and salt together. Add to liquid mixture, stir until just combined, then add green pepper, onions, and herbs. Mix quickly and lightly. Spoon into oiled muffin tins, making them two-thirds full, and top each with a cube of Gouda. Bake on middle shelf of oven at 200˚C (400˚F, gas 6) for 25 minutes. Run a knife round the edges to loosen, and remove.
Makes 12-16

> HINT
> ● *If your bread loaves or muffins won't turn out easily, let them stand for a minute or two, then run a knife around the sides and either invert or ease out.*

Bran Banana Muffins

125 g (4 oz) plain flour
pinch of salt
5 ml (1 tsp) ground cinnamon
5 ml (1 tsp) ground mixed spice
15 ml (1 tbsp) baking powder
45 g (1½ oz) bran flakes, coarsely
crushed
75 g (2½ oz) caster sugar
60 g (2 oz) soft butter
3 large, ripe bananas
1 egg
125 ml (4 fl oz) milk
25 ml (5 tsp) honey
few drops vanilla essence
45 g (1½ oz) toasted sunflower seeds
or
60 g (2 oz) chopped pecan nuts

Sift flour, salt, spices and baking powder. Mix in cereal and sugar. Rub in butter. Mash bananas and whisk together with egg, milk, honey and vanilla. Add to flour mixture together with sunflower seeds or nuts. Mix lightly until just combined and spoon into oiled muffin tins, making them two-thirds full. Bake at 200˚C (400˚F, gas 6) for 20 minutes. Stand for a few minutes before removing.
Makes 14

Overnight Muffins

125 g (4 oz) wholewheat flour
125 g (4 oz) white bread flour or
plain flour
100 g (3½ oz) caster sugar
60 ml (4 tbsp) oil
few drops vanilla essence
7.5 ml (1½ tsp) bicarbonate of soda
1 egg, beaten
1.25 ml (¼ tsp) salt
250 ml (8 fl oz) milk
5 ml (1 tsp) ground cinnamon
1.25 ml (¼ tsp) grated nutmeg
125 g (4 oz) seedless raisins
60 g (2 oz) chopped walnuts or
pecan nuts (optional)

Mix all the ingredients, except raisins and nuts. Mix these in last. Cover batter and refrigerate overnight. To bake, spoon into oiled muffin tins, making them three-quarters full. Bake at 200˚C (400˚F, gas 6) for 15-20 minutes, until well risen and browned.
Makes about 18

Honey Fruit Muffins

125 g (4 oz) plain flour
2.5 ml (½ tsp) salt
5 ml (1 tsp) bicarbonate of soda
2.5 ml (½ tsp) ground mixed spice
60 ml (4 tbsp) demerara sugar
125 g (4 oz) wholewheat flour
125 g (4 oz) seedless raisins
45 ml (3 tbsp) mixed peel
1 egg
60 ml (4 tbsp) oil
60 ml (4 tbsp) light honey
250 ml (8 fl oz) buttermilk

Sift plain flour, salt, bicarbonate of soda and spice. Mix in sugar, wholewheat flour, raisins and mixed peel. Whisk together egg, oil, honey and buttermilk. Add to dry ingredients and mix quickly to a lumpy batter. Spoon into oiled muffin tins, making them three-quarters full, and bake at 200˚C (400˚F, gas 6) for 20-22 minutes. Stand for a minute, run a knife round the edges and remove.
Makes 12 large muffins

GINGER NUT MUFFINS

250 g (9 oz) plain flour
15 ml (1 tbsp) baking powder
1.25 ml (¼ tsp) salt
10 ml (2 tsp) ground ginger
45 ml (3 tbsp) caster sugar
4 knobs preserved ginger, chopped
60 g (2 oz) chopped walnuts or
pecan nuts
60 ml (4 tbsp) oil
1 egg, beaten
125 ml (4 fl oz) milk
125 ml (4 fl oz) water
25 ml (5 tsp) ginger syrup

Sift flour, baking powder, salt and ginger. Add sugar, chopped ginger and nuts. Whisk oil, egg, milk, water and syrup together. Pour into well in centre of dry ingredients, mix quickly, using a wooden spoon. Spoon into oiled muffin tins, making them two-thirds full. Bake at 200°C (400°F, gas 6) for 20-25 minutes. Cool slightly, then remove.
Makes 12

LIGHT CHOCOLATE MUFFINS

250 g (9 oz) plain flour
15 ml (1 tbsp) baking powder
1.25 ml (¼ tsp) salt
25 ml (5 tsp) cocoa powder
75 g (2½ oz) caster sugar
60 g (2 oz) chopped walnuts or
pecan nuts
60 ml (4 tbsp) oil
1 egg, beaten
125 ml (4 fl oz) milk
125 ml (4 fl oz) water
10 ml (2 tsp) instant coffee granules

Sift flour, baking powder, salt and cocoa. Add sugar and nuts. Whisk oil, egg, milk, water and coffee granules together. Pour into well in centre of dry ingredients. Mix lightly, using a wooden spoon. Spoon into oiled muffin tins, making them two-thirds full. Bake at 200°C (400°F, gas 6) for 20-25 minutes.
Makes 12

Savoury muffins such as Cottage Cheese, Green Pepper and Onion Muffins, and Spring Onion, Cheese and Celery Muffins, go well with soup.

CHEESE AND HERB MUFFINS

Great with soups or salads.

125 g (4 oz) plain flour
20 ml (4 tsp) baking powder
2.5 ml (½ tsp) salt
5 ml (1 tsp) dry mustard
125 g (4 oz) wholewheat flour
5 ml (1 tsp) dried mixed herbs
10 ml (2 tsp) caster sugar
45 ml (3 tbsp) finely chopped parsley
100 g (3½ oz) grated Cheddar cheese
1 egg
250 ml (8 fl oz) milk
60 ml (4 tbsp) oil
extra grated cheese or sesame seeds

Sift plain flour, baking powder, salt and mustard. Mix in wholewheat flour, herbs, sugar, parsley and cheese. Beat egg with milk and oil, pour into dry mixture and mix lightly. Spoon into oiled muffin tins, making them two-thirds full. Sprinkle with extra cheese or sesame seeds and bake at 200°C (400°F, gas 6) for 25 minutes. Cool slightly, run a knife round the edges and remove. Serve with butter.
Makes 12-14

CARROT AND FRUIT MUFFINS

Add a handful of sunflower seeds or chopped walnuts for crunch.

30 g (3 oz) seedless raisins
45 ml (3 tbsp) chopped mixed peel
250 ml (8 fl oz) water
150-200 g (5-7 oz) demerara sugar
90 g (3 oz) coarsely grated carrots
30 g (1 oz) butter
5 ml (1 tsp) ground mixed spice
125 g (4 oz) plain flour
5 ml (1 tsp) bicarbonate of soda
5 ml (1 tsp) baking powder
pinch of salt
125 g (4 oz) wholewheat flour
45 g (1½ oz) desiccated coconut
few drops vanilla essence

Carrot and Fruit Muffins; Health Muffins; Coconut Currant Muffins.

Place fruit, water, sugar, carrots, butter and spice in saucepan. Bring to the boil, cover and simmer gently for 10 minutes. Cool completely. Sift plain flour, bicarbonate of soda, baking powder and salt and stir into cooled mixture. Add whole wheat flour, coconut and vanilla, and nuts if using. Spoon into oiled muffin tins, making them two-thirds full. Bake at 200°C (400°F, gas 6) for 18-20 minutes. Stand for 1 minute, then remove.
Makes 12-14

HINT
● *Wholewheat and white flours can often be interchanged; however wholewheat flour will need more liquid.*

HEALTH MUFFINS

These wholesome muffins, containing rye and wholewheat flours, will not rise quite as high as those using refined ingredients. The molasses adds colour and flavour, while the raisins and sunflower seeds provide extra nutrition.

60 g (2 oz) self-raising flour
2.5 ml (½ tsp) salt
7.5 ml (1½ tsp) baking powder
5 ml (1 tsp) ground mixed spice
90 g (3 oz) caster sugar
125 g (4 oz) wholewheat flour
60 g (2 oz) rye flour
75 g (2½ oz) seedless raisins
45 g (1½ oz) sunflower seeds
1 egg
250 ml (8 fl oz) buttermilk
20 ml (4 tsp) molasses
125 ml (4 fl oz) oil

Sift self-raising flour, salt, baking powder, spice and sugar. Mix in wholewheat and rye flours. Add raisins and sunflower seeds. Whisk together egg, buttermilk, molasses and oil. Add to flour mixture and mix lightly. Spoon into oiled muffin tins, making them two-thirds full, and bake at 200°C (400°F, gas 6) for 25 minutes.
Makes 16

NUTTY DATE MUFFINS

250 g (9 oz) stoned dates, finely chopped
45 ml (3 tbsp) mixed peel
30 g (1 oz) butter
250 ml (8 fl oz) boiling water
125 g (4 oz) plain flour
5 ml (1 tsp) baking powder
5 ml (1 tsp) bicarbonate of soda
pinch of salt
5 ml (1 tsp) ground cinnamon
1.25 ml (¼ tsp) grated nutmeg
pinch of ground cloves
125 g (4 oz) wholewheat flour
75 g (2½ oz) demerara sugar
45 g (1½ oz) chopped walnuts or pecan nuts
few drops vanilla essence
100 ml (3½ fl oz) buttermilk

Put dates, mixed peel and butter into bowl, pour boiling water over, stir to mix and then leave to cool. Sift plain flour, baking powder, bicarbonate of soda, salt and spices. Add wholewheat flour and sugar. Mix in cooled date mixture, nuts and vanilla and then quickly moisten with buttermilk. Spoon into oiled muffin tins, making them two-thirds full. Bake at 200°C (400°F, gas 6) for 15-20 minutes.
Makes 12-16

COCONUT CURRANT MUFFINS

250 g (9 oz) plain flour
15 ml (1 tbsp) baking powder
1.25 ml (¼ tsp) salt
75 g (2½ oz) caster sugar
75 g (2½ oz) desiccated coconut
60 g (2 oz) currants
60 ml (4 tbsp) oil
1 egg, beaten
125 ml (4 fl oz) milk
125 ml (4 fl oz) water
extra desiccated coconut

Sift flour, baking powder and salt. Add sugar, coconut and currants. Whisk together the oil, egg, milk and water.

Pour into well in centre of dry ingredients. Mix lightly – the batter should be lumpy. Spoon into oiled muffin tins, making them two-thirds full, sprinkle tops with coconut and bake at 200°C (400°F, gas 6) for 20-25 minutes. Cool slightly, then remove.
Makes 12

CHEESE MUFFINS

Using half milk and half water makes muffins especially light, as in these golden-brown savoury muffins – delicious served hot with butter. For added flavour, strip the leaves off a few sprigs of fresh thyme and add with the cheese.

185 ml (6½ oz) plain flour
15 ml (1 tbsp) baking powder
1.25 ml (¼ tsp) salt
5 ml (1 tsp) dry mustard
100 g (3½ oz) finely grated, mature Cheddar cheese
5 ml (1 tsp) caster sugar
75 ml (5 tbsp) milk
75 ml (5 tbsp) water
60 ml (4 tbsp) oil
1 egg
paprika and/or tiny cubes of cheese

Sift flour, baking powder, salt and mustard. Mix in cheese and sugar. Whisk together milk, water, oil and egg. Add to flour mixture and stir quickly until just combined – mixture will not be smooth. Spoon into oiled muffin tins, making them two-thirds full, and sprinkle with paprika, placing a tiny cube of cheese in the middle, if using. Bake on middle shelf of oven at 200°C (400°F, gas 6) for 25 minutes. Stand for a minute, then run a knife round the edges to loosen, and remove.
Makes 12

SCONES

BASIC FEATHERLIGHT SCONES

Scones to serve with jam and cream.

250 g (9 oz) plain flour
20 ml (4 tsp) baking powder
pinch of salt
25 ml (5 tsp) caster sugar
60 g (2 oz) soft butter
45 ml (3 tbsp) milk
45 ml (3 tbsp) water
1 egg
2.5 ml (½ tsp) lemon juice

GLAZE
1 egg yolk beaten with 5 ml (1 tsp)
water

Sift the flour, baking powder and salt together. Add sugar, then rub in butter. Beat together milk, water, egg and lemon juice. Pour into a well in the centre of the dry ingredients. Mix lightly with a fork to a soft dough, then pat out on lightly floured board. Working quickly, either cut into squares, or cut into rounds with a 6-cm (2½-in) cutter. Place on lightly oiled or non-stick baking tray. Glaze the scones with egg-wash and bake towards top of oven at 220°C (425°F, gas 7) for 12 minutes. Serve as fresh as possible.
Makes 10

GOLDEN-TOPPED CHEESE SCONES

250 g (9 oz) plain flour or white bread flour
20 ml (4 tsp) baking powder
2.5 ml (½ tsp) dry mustard
1.25 ml (¼ tsp) salt
pinch of cayenne pepper
100 g (3½ oz) grated Cheddar cheese
45 ml (3 tbsp) oil
1 egg
45 ml (3 tbsp) milk
45 ml (3 tbsp) water

Basic Featherlight Scones;
Spicy Raisin Scones (page 73).

TOPPING
25 ml (5 tsp) melted butter
45 g (1½ oz) grated Cheddar cheese
2.5 ml (½ tsp) Marmite

Sift together flour, baking powder, mustard, salt and cayenne. Add cheese. Beat together oil, egg, milk and water. Pour into a well in centre of dry ingredients and mix lightly with a fork until dough holds together. Pat out 2-cm (¾-in) thick on lightly floured board, cut into rounds with 6-cm (2½-in) scone cutter and place on oiled baking tray.

Mash together ingredients for topping and place a teaspoonful on top of each scone. Bake towards top of oven at 220°C (425°F, gas 7) for 12 minutes. Serve hot with butter.
Makes 10-12

DROPPED CHEESE SCONES

Exceptionally light and quickly-made scones, requiring no cutting; delicious served hot with butter for tea or a special breakfast.

250 g (9 oz) plain flour
15 ml (1 tbsp) baking powder
5 ml (1 tsp) sugar
1.25 ml (¼ tsp) salt
5 ml (1 tsp) dry mustard
45 g (1½ oz) grated mature Cheddar cheese
1 egg
100 ml (3½ fl oz) milk
100 ml (3½ fl oz) water
45 ml (3 tbsp) oil
paprika

Sift the flour, baking powder, sugar, salt and dry mustard. Add the cheese. Beat the egg, milk, water and oil together. Make a well in the centre of the dry ingredients and pour in the liquid. Mix quickly to a soft dough, using a fork. Drop spoonfuls on to an oiled baking tray, lightly dust the tops with paprika and bake towards the top of the oven at 220°C (425°F, gas 7) for 10-12 minutes.
Makes 12

SOURED CREAM, SAGE AND CHIVE SCONES

A delicious, savoury scone. If fresh herbs are not available, 5 ml (1 tsp) dried mixed herbs may be substituted.

250 g (9 oz) self-raising flour
1.25 ml (¼ tsp) salt
10 ml (2 tsp) caster sugar
125 ml (4 fl oz) soured cream
25 ml (5 tsp) finely chopped chives
16 fresh sage leaves, finely chopped
45 ml (3 tbsp) finely chopped parsley
1 egg
45 ml (3 tbsp) water
milk and poppy seeds

Sift flour, salt and sugar. Mix in soured cream and herbs. Beat egg with water and add, mixing to a soft dough. Turn on to floured board and pat out 2-cm (¾-in) thick. Cut into squares, or into rounds, using a 6-cm (2½-in) floured cutter and being careful not to twist when cutting. Place on oiled baking tray, brush with milk and sprinkle with poppy seeds. Bake towards top of oven at 220°C (425°F, gas 7) for 12 minutes. Serve hot.
Makes 8-10

FAT-FREE SCONES

Made without eggs or butter.

250 g (9 oz) self-raising flour
1.25 ml (¼ tsp) salt
20 ml (4 tsp) caster sugar
45 ml (3 tbsp) fat-free milk powder
150 ml (¼ pint) water
60 ml (4 tbsp) oil

Sift flour, salt and sugar together. Mix milk powder into water and beat together with oil. Add to flour mixture and mix lightly. Pat out 2-cm (¾-in) thick on a lightly floured board and cut, using a 6-cm (2½ in) cutter. Place on oiled baking tray and bake towards top of oven at 220°C (425°F, gas 7) for 12 minutes. Serve hot, with butter and cheese, or jam.
Makes 10

WHOLEWHEAT FRUIT SCONES

Hearty wedges of fruity goodness.

125 g (4 oz) white bread flour
20 ml (4 tsp) baking powder
2.5 ml (½ tsp) salt
185 g (6½ oz) wholewheat flour
125 g (4 oz) mixed dried fruit
25 ml (5 tsp) demerara sugar
5 ml (1 tsp) finely grated orange rind
(optional)
1 egg
75 ml (5 tbsp) milk
75 ml (5 tbsp) water
25 ml (5 tsp) honey
75 ml (5 tbsp) oil

TOPPING
10 ml (2 tsp) caster sugar
2.5 ml (½ tsp) ground cinnamon

Sift the white bread flour, baking powder and salt together. Add wholewheat flour, fruit, sugar and rind. Beat egg, milk, water, honey and oil together and pour into well in centre of dry ingredients. Using a fork, mix quickly to a soft dough. Pat out into a round on a lightly floured board, brush with egg glaze or milk, and sprinkle with topping. Using a sharp knife, cut into 8-10 wedges and place on oiled baking tray. Bake just above centre of oven at 220°C (425°F, gas 7) for 15-18 minutes.
Makes 8-10 wedges

GINGER SCONES

250 g (9 oz) plain flour
20 ml (4 tsp) baking powder
1.25 ml (¼ tsp) salt
25 ml (5 tsp) caster sugar
5 ml (1 tsp) ground ginger
60 g (2 oz) butter
3-4 large knobs preserved
ginger, finely chopped
45 ml (3 tbsp) mixed peel, finely
chopped
60 ml (4 tbsp) milk
60 ml (4 tbsp) water
1 egg

Sift dry ingredients. Rub in butter. Add chopped ginger and mixed peel. Beat together milk, water and egg. Add to dry ingredients and mix lightly with a fork to a soft ball. Pat out 2-cm (¾-in) thick on floured board – you may have to flour your hands a little – and cut into 6-cm (2½-in) rounds, or squares, or triangles. Place on oiled baking tray and bake towards top of oven at 220°C (425°F, gas 7) for 12 minutes.
Makes about 12

NOTE
● *A dash of lemon juice added to the liquid will lighten scones. When using a scone cutter, be careful not to twist when you cut out the scones.*

PUMPKIN SCONES

Serve these scones with butter and honey. Use a bright orange, firm-fleshed pumpkin, and drain well after cooking.

60 g (2 oz) soft butter
100 g (3½ oz) demerara sugar
1 egg, lightly beaten
375 g (13 oz) self-raising flour
2.5 ml (½ tsp) salt
10 ml (2 tsp) ground ginger
5 ml (1 tsp) ground cinnamon
pinch of ground cloves
75 g (2½ oz) seedless raisins
250 ml (8 fl oz) smooth
pumpkin purée
45 ml (3 tbsp) chopped mixed peel

Cream butter and sugar. Beat in egg, adding 5 ml (1 tsp) of the flour. Sift flour, salt and spices and add. Mix well. Add raisins, pumpkin and mixed peel. Mix to a soft dough – no liquid is required, as the purée should moisten the mixture sufficiently. Pat out 2-cm (¾-in) thick on to floured board and cut into rounds, using a floured 6-cm (2½-in) cutter. Place on oiled baking tray and brush tops with egg glaze. Bake just above centre of oven at 220°C for 12 minutes.
Makes 14-16

WHOLEWHEAT CHEESE SCONES

125 g (4 oz) white bread flour
15 ml (1 tbsp) baking powder
1.25 ml (¼ tsp) salt
10 ml (2 tsp) caster sugar
5 ml (1 tsp) dry mustard
125 g (4 oz) wholewheat flour
45 g (1½ oz) butter
100g (3½ oz) grated Cheddar cheese
1 egg
45 ml (3 tbsp) milk
45 ml (3 tbsp) water

GLAZE
1 egg yolk beaten with 5 ml (1 tsp)
water
paprika

Sift white flour, baking powder, salt, sugar and mustard. Add wholewheat flour, rub in butter, then add cheese. Beat egg, milk and water together and add. Mix with a fork and then lightly form into a ball, adding, if necessary, 5-10 ml (1-2 tsp) water. Pat out on lightly floured board and cut into nine squares. Place on oiled baking tray. Brush with egg wash, sprinkle with paprika and bake towards top of oven at 220°C (425°F, gas 7) for 12 minutes. Serve hot with butter and honey.
Makes 9

SPICY FRUIT SCONES

Sweet tea-time scones.

250 g (9 oz) self-raising flour
1.25 ml (¼ tsp) salt
5 ml (1 tsp) ground mixed spice
25 ml (5 tsp) sugar
60 g (2 oz) soft butter
90g (3 oz) mixed dried fruit
1 egg
45 ml (3 tbsp) milk
45 ml (3 tbsp) water

TOPPING
milk
5 ml (1 tsp) sugar
2.5 ml (½ tsp) ground cinnamon

Sift flour, salt and spice. Add sugar and rub in butter. Add dried fruit. Beat egg, milk and water. Pour into a well in centre of dry ingredients and mix lightly with a fork. When thoroughly combined, pat out on lightly floured board and cut into squares or rounds, using a 6-cm (2½-in) cutter. Place on oiled baking tray, brush with milk and sprinkle with sugar mixed with cinnamon. Bake just above centre of oven at 220°C (425°F, gas 7) for 12 minutes.
Makes 10

> **NOTE**
> ● *Instead of breaking an egg just for glazing, milk may be substituted, but the resulting scone or loaf will not have the same rich brown colour.*

JIFFY SCONES

Light, white scones that rise like little stuffed pillows, especially if cut into squares instead of rounds. Remember that cutters, if twisted, will frighten the life out of scones. These scones may be served with either sweet or savoury things.

250 g (9 oz) self-raising flour
1.25 ml (¼ tsp) salt
15 ml (1 tbsp) caster sugar
1 egg
60 ml (4 tbsp) oil
buttermilk
milk or egg-wash

Sift the flour, salt and sugar together. Break the egg into a measuring jug. Add the oil and enough buttermilk to fill the jug to the 200-ml (7-fl oz) mark. Whisk well, then add to dry ingredients. Mix quickly, using a fork, until mixture holds together, then toss into a ball with your hands. Pat out 2-cm (¾-in) thick on lightly floured board, and cut into desired shapes. Place on oiled baking tray, brush with milk or egg-wash, and bake just above centre of oven at 220°C (425°F, gas 7) for 12 minutes.
Makes about 10

Golden-topped Cheese Scones; Jiffy Scones; Soured Cream, Sage and Chive Scones.

SPICY RAISIN SCONES

125 g (4 oz) plain flour
20 ml (4 tsp) baking powder
2.5 ml (½ tsp) salt
45 ml (3 tbsp) caster sugar
5 ml (1 tsp) ground mixed spice
125 g (4 oz) wholewheat flour
125 g (4 oz) seedless raisins
1 egg
60 ml (4 tbsp) milk
60 ml (4 tbsp) water
60 ml (4 tbsp) oil

TOPPING
milk
5 ml (1 tsp) caster sugar
5 ml (1 tsp) ground cardamom or cinnamon

Sift the plain flour, baking powder, sugar, spice and salt together. Add the wholewheat flour and raisins and toss until coated. Whisk the egg, milk, water and oil together. Pour all at once into a well in the centre of the dry ingredients and, using a fork, mix to a soft dough. As soon as the mixture holds together, turn out onto a lightly floured board. Pat the dough out until 2-cm (¾-in) thick. The dough will be soft, therefore you should flour a 6-cm (2½-in) cutter before cutting out rounds. Arrange the scones on an oiled baking tray, brush the tops with milk and sprinkle with sugar and spice. Bake just above the centre of the oven at 220°C (425°F, gas 7) for 12 minutes.
Makes 12

YEAST BREADS

Bread-baking is a long and involved story, dating right back to the Stone Age, when grain was crushed between two stones, mixed to a dough with water, shaped into thin cakes and baked on a stone over a fire. As can be imagined, these bread cakes were hard and very chewy. The triumph of discovering 'risen' bread is ascribed to a forgetful Egyptian, who mixed some dough and then went off somewhere on his camel, leaving the dough sitting in the hot sun – whereupon it fermented, and rose. Another, more plausible story, is that they learnt to use the yeasty foam from the top of their fermenting wines.

In due course the Egyptians grew so much wheat that they were able to export it. The Greeks bought much of the grain, and were so quick to develop the art of baking beautiful breads that they became the master bakers of the period. The skill was further developed by the conquering Romans, who eventually introduced their knowledge to Britain. It is said that Cassius was so appalled by the quality of the bread he found on his arrival in Britain, that he immediately signalled his baker in Rome to send him some that he could eat.

It took many centuries before proper mills were developed and bread became a commodity within everyone's reach. Today, of course, due to mechanization, bread in all its forms is available everywhere.

Basically, bread is made from flour, yeast, salt and liquid, and kneading it allows the gluten in the flour to stretch and form an elastic framework around the gas bubbles from the yeast.

Flour: There are four main types of wheat flour widely available for bread-baking. White bread or strong flour is used for most white breads. It has a high gluten content, and produces loaves of a creamy colour. Plain white flour is highly refined and produces finely textured, fluffy rolls; it may also be used for very light breads. Brown bread flour has had the coarsest bran removed and produces light brown loaves with a good volume. Wholewheat (wholemeal) flour has a high percentage of bran and wheat germ. Bread made from this flour is dark in colour, has a slightly nutty flavour and a dense coarse texture. Flours made from other grains, like rye, have very little gluten and should always be mixed with another flour. Soya flour is rich in protein, and helps bread to remain fresh and moist. Both with regard to rising times and the amount of water absorbed, please be prepared to adapt; there are few hard and fast rules and it really is a matter of trial and perception. Sometimes a dough will 'draw' together quickly into a ball – at other times you could add the same amount of water and find it looks flaky. Different flours vary as to absorption capacity, and this must be borne in mind. Nevertheless, yeast cookery should be tackled with confidence and enthusiasm. Short of not activating the yeast by using water that is too cool, or killing it with water that is too hot, if it is properly kneaded it will eventually spring up. Yeast is tougher than one thinks; the water should be warm rather than cool.

Yeast: Yeast is a living substance composed of tiny cells. When provided with moisture, food and warmth, the cells grow and give off carbon dioxide, which causes the dough to rise. Yeast also gives off alcohol, which is driven off by the heat of the oven, but which can give the dough a sour taste if left to rise for too long. And please do not think that by using more yeast you will get a better rise – the bread will simply taste yeasty. Yeast should not be hurried and, given time, even relatively small quantities will rise heavy doughs.

For the sake of convenience, I have used dried yeast in all recipes requiring yeast. It is available in sachets as well as tins and, unlike compressed yeast, it keeps well — although once opened it is best to store it, sealed, in the refrigerator. Instant dry yeast is sold in sachets and has a long shelf life, but should be used right away once opened.

When dissolving dried yeast, the water temperature is most important. If it is too hot, the yeast cells will be killed; if too cold, they will not grow. A little warmer than lukewarm is about right, but experience remains the best teacher. A little sugar is usually added to the water as food for the yeast, and the yeast is then sprinkled on to the surface. Do not stir, but leave it to froth, and then just before adding it to the flour, give it a quick stir to make sure that all the granules have dissolved.

Liquid: Water is, naturally, the easiest liquid to use and provides the best volume and will result in a thick, crisp crust. The addition of milk, however, will make the bread more nutritious and it also improves the texture of the crumb and results in a softer crust. I always scald the milk first, and then leave to cool to lukewarm – scalding destroys bacteria and makes the dough somewhat easier to handle. The amount of liquid added to a dough varies, depending on the type of flour used. Start with the specified amount, and if the dough appears flaky, make further small additions until the required elasticity is reached. Once kneaded, further liquid cannot be successfully added, although extra flour can be incorporated into a too-soft dough.

Salt: Bread without salt is not palatable, but it should be used with discretion. Salt prevents the yeast from fermenting too quickly, thereby providing a good texture due to a slower rising, but too much of it will kill the yeast and then it won't rise at all. Too little salt results in a coarse crumb.

Sugar: Apart from being a food for the yeast, sugar also gives colour to the crust. Because it slows down the fermentation process, sweet yeast loaves require a longer rising period than plain breads. Remember that too much sugar will produce a poorly risen loaf.

Shortening: Butter, margarine or lard are regarded as the best shortenings for improving keeping qualities, increasing volume, and adding to the flavour and softness of crumb. Oil may also be used, especially in the baking of 'health' breads, but it does nothing for the colour of the loaf.

Eggs: These are sometimes added to enrich and colour the bread. Breads containing eggs also have a much more tender crust.

Dried fruit, cheese, vegetables: The addition of these makes the dough heavier and involves a longer rising period.

Kneading: Turn the dough out on to a lightly floured board and be prepared for a 10 minute session. I do not think one can ever over-knead a dough, and under-kneading will have an undesirable result – so roll up your sleeves and punch away. The idea is to fold the dough over and then push it down and away with the heels of your palms; turn it slightly – I find an anti-clockwise movement comes most naturally – and then fold and press down again. On and on. It becomes quite hypnotic eventually, especially when the dough starts responding by becoming smooth and soft and pliable, without being sticky. If it does feel sticky, sprinkle a little extra flour on the board and carry on – if necessary sprinkle on more flour, but do so a little at a time so that you don't make it too stiff, in which case the dough cannot 'balloon'.

Rising: In order to avoid a crust forming on top of the dough, brush the mixing bowl with oil, turn the dough in it to coat the top, then cover. Another method is to cover the bowl with a damp cloth. The dough is then left to rise in a warm, draught-free place. Rising times vary, depending on the temperature in your kitchen – in cold weather it will, of course, take longer. Rising times are also affected by the amount of yeast, the kind of flour, and the extra ingredients used. I like to put the bowl in the warming drawer of my oven. Turn it on briefly beforehand and then turn it off again. If the dough is allowed to get too hot, the bread will be coarse and will break. As a general rule, the dough should double in volume. If allowed to over-prove, the loaf will have a coarse texture and poor flavour, while under-proving produces a heavy loaf with a loose top.

Second rising or proving: Once doubled, punch the dough down by pushing your fist into the middle, turn it inwards and over, and knead again for a minute or two to break up the pockets of gas. For really fine-textured bread, it may be left to rise again – but this is time-consuming. Alternatively, either shape the dough immediately, or better still, cover and let it rest for 10 minutes, and then shape and cover. Oiled plastic wrap is convenient because it does not lie heavily on the dough. Do not cover tightly – leave space for air to circulate. Leave to rise until doubled in volume, or nearly doubled in some cases, once again in a warming drawer or other warm spot.

Glazing: Breads and rolls are usually glazed just before baking and, although egg-wash is often recommended, especially when baking rolls, I usually use milk – breaking an egg just for glazing seems an unnecessary extravagance and milk or water or a sugar-water solution are all satisfactory. Coarsely crushed wheat, sesame, sunflower and poppy seeds, all make attractive finishes. With certain breads or rolls a pan of boiling water may be placed on the bottom shelf of the oven to encourage a shiny, crisp crust.

Baking: Even with sweet breads, which are usually baked at lower temperatures than other breads, I like to start off with a hot oven in order to stop the fermentation of the yeast. Exact temperatures and positioning in the oven are specified with each recipe – it is important to abide by them to avoid over-browning. To test whether a loaf (or a roll) is cooked, turn it over and knock on the bottom – it should sound distinctly hollow. If in doubt, return to the oven, out of the tin and upside down, for a short while at a lower temperature. Always cool bread completely on a wire rack before storing.

Mishaps: Here again experience is the best teacher and the more you bake with yeast, the sooner you will learn the reason for imperfect results and how to avoid them. However, a few pointers may help. The greatest mistakes are in making a dough too wet or too dry, under- or over-proving, and insufficient kneading. These will result in loaves that have poor volume, an uneven shape, heavy texture, holes and a coarse crumb, with a crust that either breaks at the sides, or is very thick and has a poor crumb colour. Over-risen dough, especially in too warm a place, also results in a strong yeast taste. Using a tin of the wrong size also spells disaster to the shape of a loaf – if the tin is too small you'll end up with an irregular shape and a cracked crust. Frankly, there's such a long list of possible faults that it is best just to follow the recipes carefully, remembering the main points I have listed, and the importance of the correct temperature – both in dissolving the yeast, rising and proving, and finally, in baking.

Shaping breads: The traditional loaf-tin bread has great appeal. Press the dough into a rectangle and then fold inwards from each side. Drop into the tin with the seam underneath. A farmhouse-style loaf may be made by slashing the top lengthwise, creating a sunburst effect. Plaits are also most effective – divide the dough into three, roll into sausages and plait – but not too tightly. Cobs are made by shaping the dough into a round ball, then flattening it slightly before placing on a floured sheet, proving and then sprinkling the top with flour before baking. Cottage loaves are made in the same way as cottage rolls, but are larger. A bloomer loaf is a long loaf with blunt ends and a flat top, fatter than a French loaf, and slashed on top before proving. When proving these loaves, which are not placed in tins, it is a good idea to support the sides with crumpled tea-towels so that they do not spread sideways too much. Tins other than loaf tins may be used, such as ring tins, or round cake tins, as in crown loaves. These are amongst the most attractive of breads: the dough is shaped into rolls, and arranged round the circumference of the tin, with one roll in the middle. They are then topped with grated cheese, sesame or poppy seeds. In proving and baking, these rolls join to form a 'crown' of humped buns.

SWEET YEAST BREADS

Although these are not as straightforward as ordinary breads, the different shapes and decorations are fun to make. I have included a few recipes, mostly of Continental origin, where they are most popular. Due to the addition of 'heavy' ingredients they will take longer to rise and prove, and although they are usually baked at a lower temperature because they brown more quickly, I like to start them off at a high temperature, as I said, to kill the yeast, and then reduce the temperature after about 10 minutes. They are usually baked towards the top of the oven. Sweet yeast breads may either be decorated before baking, or left to cool, and simply iced. They go stale quite quickly, and may then be toasted.

ROLLS

Rolls are baked at a high temperature towards the top of the oven, and eaten fresh. Experiment with different shapes – round rolls; sausage-shaped finger rolls; snails, twists and knots, which are made by rolling the dough into long thin sausages; cottage rolls, in which a small ball of dough is placed on top of a larger round and secured by pushing your finger through the centre; and crescents, which, like croissants, are shaped by rolling a triangle up from the long end and twisting into a horseshoe.

RUSKS

I have included kneaded rusks and 'easy' rusks – both good and lovely for dunking. It is important, when separating rusks, not to slice them as this does affect the flavour. It is fine to use a knife as an aid, but it is better to use the tines of a fork. Whatever you do, always try to break them through, and dry them out on baking trays in a very low oven or warming drawer so that they end up crisped without browning.

QUICK BREADS

Whether sweet or savoury, these are great time-savers and require no rising times as they are made with self-raising flour, baking powder, or bicarbonate of soda and cream of tartar. Cheese and/or nuts are often used in these loaves, and it is useful to have a ready-grated or chopped supply available. I grate large quantities of cheese in my food processor, using the grinding blade, and then store it in plastic bags in my freezer. The same applies to nuts, but be careful not to grind them too finely, otherwise the end product will not have the same texture. Sweet quick loaves are often more flavoursome if left for a day or two before slicing.

SCONES

It goes without saying that scones should always be eaten fresh. They are baked at a high temperature, towards the top of the oven. It is preferable not to roll them out before cutting – patting is better – to ensure lightness, and if using a cutter, be sure not to twist as you cut, as they will not rise as they should. A dash of lemon juice will also help to lighten scones.

MUFFINS

The golden rule here is never to over-mix; muffin batter will usually be lumpy rather than smooth. Never over-fill tins as they will rise over the sides and be difficult to remove. As with scones, break, rather than slice them in half before buttering.

BISCUITS

I have tried to keep the time expended in biscuit-making to a minimum because few of us, these days, can indulge in rolling and cutting and baking tray after tray of biscuits as they used to do in granny's time, and so I have included many recipes for biscuits that are simply rolled into balls. There are also some refrigerator biscuits, which only need to be sliced once chilled, and bar biscuits, which are especially convenient when it comes to speed – but do try to use the size of tin recommended so that the biscuits are neither too thick nor too thin. (Incidentally, the term 'biscuit' used to be reserved for a dry, twice-baked, flour and water mixture, but today, cookies – which are quite different in texture and flavour – are also sometimes called biscuits.) Using soft (not melted) butter when creaming a biscuit mixture makes the job much easier and ensures successful results. Insufficient creaming can result in a mixture that is too dry to shape, so here the electric beater comes in useful.

Shortening: I have included several recipes using oil instead of butter to cope with differing tastes and budgets. This will also make them more suitable for low-cholesterol diets. These biscuits are sometimes more difficult to handle, but are well worth attempting, and are often the crispest and most economical. I also find oil best for greasing tins and trays for all baking. Whenever possible, and especially in the case of biscuits rich in butter, position the trays on the middle shelf of the oven, to avoid over-browning on the bottom; if time allows, it is therefore better to bake biscuits in relays. Certain nutritious and unrefined ingredients have been introduced in several of the recipes, because it has been my experience that these are becoming increasingly popular, especially with teenagers.

Storing: Once cooled on wire racks, biscuits should be stored in airtight containers. It is a good idea, in the case of crisp biscuits, to sprinkle each layer with a little sugar to keep them crunchy.

INDEX